CONTENTS

LIVERPOOL FC
CARLING CUP WINNERS 2012

© Published in Great Britain in 2012 by Trinity Mirror Sport Media, PO Box 48, Old Hall Street, Liverpool L69 3EB.

ISBN: 9781908695116

Photographic credits: Trinity Mirror, Getty Images, PA Pics
Executive Editor: Ken Rogers
Senior Editor: Steve Hanrahan
Senior Art Editor: Rick Cooke
Senior Production Editor: Paul Dove
Magazine Editor: Roy Gilfoyle
Sub Editor: Adam Oldfield
Writers: Chris McLoughlin, John Hynes, Simon Hughes, William Hughes, Michael McGuinness
Design: Colin Sumpter, Alison Barkley, Lisa Critchley, Graeme Helliwell, James Kenyon
Cover Design: Rick Cooke

KENNY DALGLISH:

"I don't think anyone who has ever won a trophy has come away from it saying they didn't enjoy it.

"If you do something and you enjoy it, you are going to want more of it. It is logical.

"The idea six years ago was not to go six years without winning a trophy.

"We are where we are now because of the work everyone has done, not just me.

"The owners, the supporters, the players, everyone has chipped in. We have said that all along. The closer we are, the stronger we will be together.

"The game had to be settled some way and we feel for Anthony Gerrard, who missed the vital one that meant we won the trophy,.

"Although we have won something today, that is not us finished. We don't want to stop here, we want to keep going.

"It (Liverpool) means an awful lot to a lot of people.

"All we do is try to make them as happy as we possibly can. Today we have been able to do that. Hopefully it makes up for some of the days when we have not been able to."

'ALTHOUGH WE HAVE WON SOMETHING TODAY, THAT IS NOT US FINISHED. WE DON'T WANT TO STOP HERE, WE WANT TO KEEP GOING.'

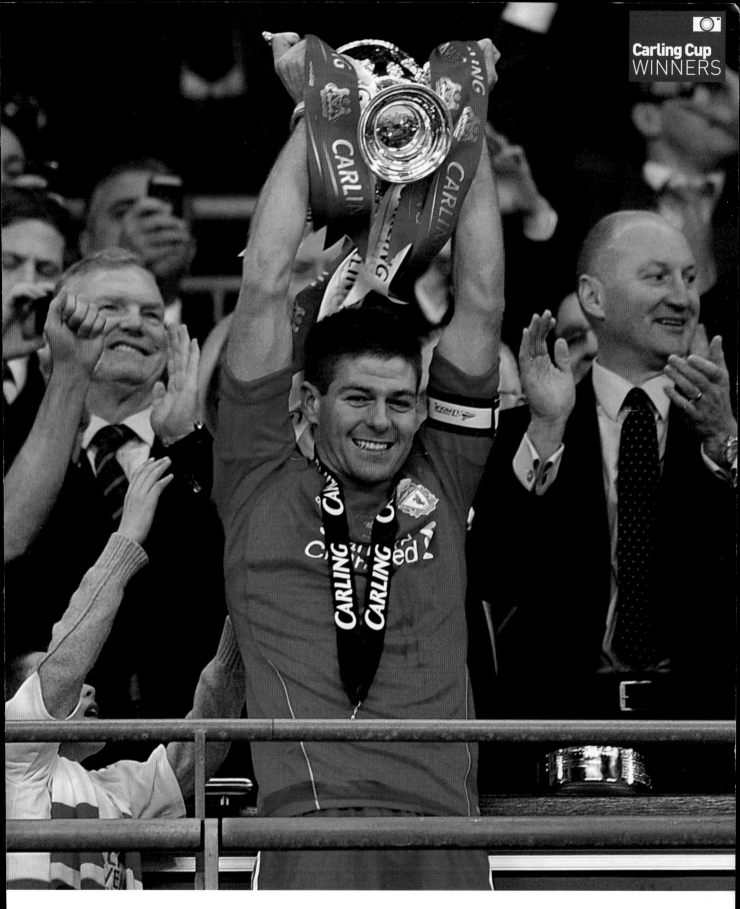

STEVEN GERRARD:

"We won't accept just this, we need more, we want more.

"It is always cruel when it goes to penalties. It was always going to be the case that one of us was going to be sad and one of us was going to be celebrating.

'Obviously, I am delighted to have won the trophy but I feel for Anthony and Cardiff. It doesn't matter what I say to him. I know that he will be down."

'IT IS ALWAYS CRUEL WHEN IT GOES TO PENALTIES. IT WAS ALWAYS GOING TO BE THE CASE THAT ONE OF US WAS GOING TO BE SAD AND ONE OF US WAS GOING TO BE CELEBRATING.'

'THE KEY IS THAT WE ACCOMPLISHED SOMETHING AS A CLUB AND FOR OUR FANS. I'M JUST PROUD WE WON BECAUSE IT'S A FIRST STEP AND WE'RE LOOKING FORWARD TO MORE SILVER.'

TOM WERNER:

"The key is that we accomplished something as a club and for our fans. I'm just proud we won because it's a first step and we're looking forward to more silver.

"I really have to pinch myself. To all of our supporters, they've seen a remarkable football match. I thought we were the better team and I'm so proud of the club and so excited for all those fans around the world who watched.

"I really couldn't watch the penalties. I heard but I couldn't watch. It's certainly at the very top (of what I've ever achieved), and to go into that dressing room and see the joy those players had: it's a memory we have and want to share with our fans."

JOHN HENRY:

"I was doing better than Tom. Tom was under the seat, he couldn't watch. This is the first step for this club in trying to get to the point where we're talking about things on the field rather than off the field. It's been going on for so many years now that it was time for the club to step up and win a big match like this.

"Just getting here: beating Chelsea at Stamford Bridge on two days' rest, to beat Manchester City over two legs - it was a tremendous accomplishment just to get here. Even if we'd lost I would have felt we'd accomplished a lot, but we didn't. It doesn't matter how you win if you win.

"The whole club had a lot of pressure but Kenny has been extraordinary from day one."

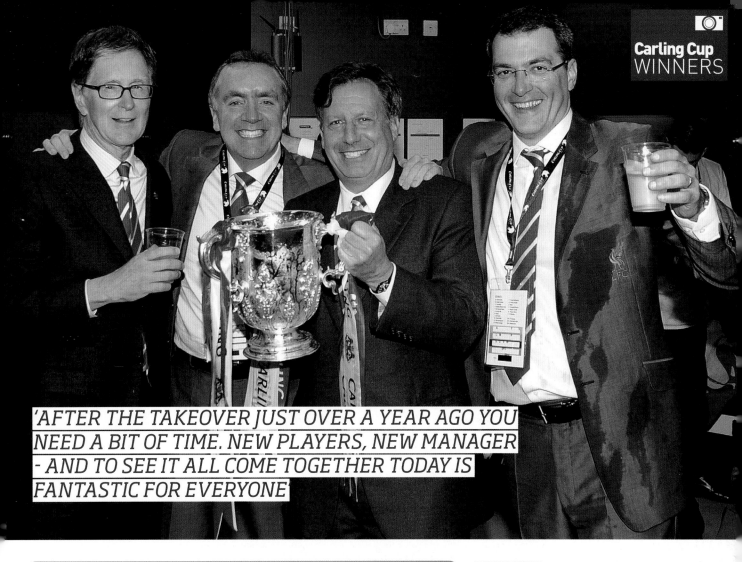

'AFTER THE TAKEOVER JUST OVER A YEAR AGO YOU NEED A BIT OF TIME. NEW PLAYERS, NEW MANAGER - AND TO SEE IT ALL COME TOGETHER TODAY IS FANTASTIC FOR EVERYONE'

IAN AYRE:

"After the takeover just over a year ago you need a bit of time. New players, new manager - and to see it all come together today is fantastic for everyone.

"For someone to come in during a pretty distressed situation and invest what they have and keep the faith, they deserve this and even more than this. They put so much into it.

"I'm really pleased for them. To see them smiling, and they now understand what extra-time and penalties means!

"We've always said that the most important thing is that we keep progressing. In the last couple of months we've seemed to progress. We've had some good results in this competition and in the league and FA Cup.

"To progress from this? Winning other trophies is what that means, I guess. We're guaranteed a place in Europe now, which is where we belong, and we can now try to push on in the FA Cup and try to get into the Champions League. As long as we keep progressing, that's what we've always said."

WEMBLEY DRAMA ENDS IN CHEERS

CARLING CUP FINAL 2012

CARLING CUP FINAL 2012

SUCCESSFUL spot-kicks from Dirk Kuyt, Stewart Downing and Glen Johnson helped Kenny Dalglish's side to win the Carling Cup on penalties during a drama filled afternoon at Wembley.

The contest needed to be decided from 12 yards after 120 minutes of pulsating action had produced a thrilling 2-2 draw.

Liverpool dominated possession and chances throughout; but Cardiff initially went ahead through Joe Mason before equalising in the last minute of extra-time thanks to a scrambled Ben Tuner effort.

In between those strikes, Martin Skrtel and Kuyt found the net to turn a deficit into a one-goal advantage.

The drama began early. Two minutes in, Glen Johnson's curling effort from the edge of the box evaded Tom Heaton before crashing down off the bar. It bounced agonisingly away from the lurking Luis Suarez, before Steven Gerrard smashed the rebound over.

Liverpool went close again when Andy Carroll headed Jordan Henderson's cross over.

Cardiff's first real attack came after some intricate passing; a neat flick by

CARDIFF CITY 2 LIVERPOOL 2
(LIVERPOOL WIN 3-2 ON PENS AET)
Wembley Stadium, 26.02.2012
Carling Cup final

Don Cowie found Kenny Miller and he lashed at the opportunity when he should have worked Pepe Reina.

Instead it was Heaton who was next in action on 18 minutes, as patient play by Henderson and Suarez led to Carroll heading down and the keeper palming away. Within seconds the Welsh side were ahead.

A quick counter-attack concluded with a fine pass by Miller to release Joe Mason, who slid the ball under Reina as he rushed out.

In the minutes that immediately followed the opener, Liverpool continued to control proceedings.

Nobody was arriving when Downing delivered a fine low cross, before Jose Enrique's right-footed effort went wide and a Charlie Adam drive finished just the wrong side of the post.

Great combination between

PLAYER WATCH

STEVEN GERRARD:

1 Receives his first touch from a Glen Johnson throw-in and plays a cushioned pass back to the full-back.

2 Takes a short pass from Jordan Henderson in his own half and drives forward towards the Cardiff box. He feeds Stewart Downing on the left. As the move develops, Johnson hits the crossbar and Gerrard follows up to drive the rebound over the bar with a volley on the run.

6 Takes first corner of game which a Cardiff player heads behind for another flag kick.

10 Exchanges passes with Luis Suarez, then feeds the Uruguayan again with a ball that has him turning and running at goal.

11 Finds Henderson on the right, then crosses into the box and Kevin McNaughton heads behind at the back post to concede another corner.

21 Passes to Daniel Agger who strides out of defence to the edge of the Cardiff box before hitting a shot on the stretch which is blocked.

30 Finds Suarez with a quick pass into the Cardiff penalty area.

38 Downing stands up a cross to the near post and when Henderson misses his shot, it runs to Gerrard at the back post but as he takes it first time, he is slightly off balance and stabs his effort over the bar.

43 His free-kick from the left picks out Agger whose header is saved by Tom Heaton though a linesman also flags for offside.

44 Receives a pass from Downing in the box and after his first shot is blocked by the chest of Andrew Taylor, his second – at full stretch – clears the crossbar.

46 After the interval, takes a free-kick which is half cleared to Henderson, but his team-mate's shot from the edge of the area goes well wide.

57 Heads away a Taylor cross into the Liverpool box.

69 Tries to play a one-two with Suarez on the edge of the Cardiff box. The Uruguayan appears to be fouled but no award is forthcoming from the officials.

74 A powerful header finds Carroll whose flick-on almost releases Suarez.

77 Picks out Downing on the edge of box and his England team-mate's deflected effort brings out a fine diving save from Heaton.

85 Finds Craig Bellamy on the right with a pinpoint pass.

86 Takes a corner on the right from which Suarez heads wide.

89 Drills in a low shot after being found 25-yards from goal by Enrique.

91 A late chance as Johnson finds the captain just outside the 'D' on the edge of the box, but his attempted curler has too much height.

EXTRA-TIME

92 Fires over the bar from outside the box after being found by a low pass from Enrique.

94 His free-kick picks out Suarez's run to the near post and he flicks a shot goalwards but is flagged offside.

104 Puts Liverpool on to the front foot with a ball into Bellamy in the Cardiff half.

107 Celebrates as Dirk Kuyt puts the Reds in front.

112 Sets Suarez away on the right with a measured pass to relieve some Cardiff pressure.

120 The game ends 2-2 after extra-time. A penalty shoot-out will decide the destiny of the trophy.

PENALTIES

6.38pm Wins the toss with Peter Whittingham for the choice of ends for the shoot-out before stepping up to take the first kick but sees it brilliantly tipped onto the bar.

6.43pm Sees his cousin Anthony miss the decisive kick for Cardiff.

6.50pm Leads the players up the steps to the Royal Box.

6.53pm Lifts the Carling Cup to chants of 'Steve Gerrard, Gerrard' from the Liverpool fans.

Downing, Carroll and Suarez almost put the number nine in on goal, only for a fine tackle by Mark Hudson to thwart the attack.

The same familiar pattern of Liverpool going forward continued as the interval edged nearer.

Downing again caused danger with another threatening cross. Henderson was well positioned but mis-kicked, before Gerrard was off target with the follow-up.

Suarez worked some space for himself but his effort from the edge of the area was comfortably gathered by Heaton.

Gerrard was next to attempt a leveller, Andrew Taylor throwing his body in the way of the skipper's shot in superb fashion.

Despite being behind, Dalglish would have been content with the performance as the teams made their way to the dressing room at the interval. The problem was the scoreboard.

'Don't become frustrated' would have been the Reds' message to each other as they emerged for the second half before their Championship opponents.

Immediately they were again pushing forward, a Gerrard free-kick only half cleared before Henderson volleyed wide.

That was the signal for Craig Bellamy to warm up to loud applause in front of the Liverpool fans.

His home-town team may have been lacking possession, yet they were still a threat, as neat build up by Cowie created room for Miller to shoot across goal. Reina's angry remonstrations indicated what he thought.

Again the action moved to the other end. Suarez's cross-shot from a tight angle was palmed away by Heaton.

CARLING CUP FINAL MATCH REPORT

A series of corners ensued, Cardiff strongly repelling each effort each time.

Carroll's flick then sent Suarez away, the Uruguayan cutting inside only for a brilliant Kevin McNaughton tackle to halt him. In such circumstances, surely a leveller would materialise. Dalglish tried to prompt it by sending on Bellamy and, within seconds, parity arrived.

Skrtel, forward for yet another set-piece, was the scorer, side-footing in after Carroll's header towards goal was nodded against the post by Suarez.

Suddenly all the noise inside the stadium was emanating from the red end. Some Suarez trickery in the box saw him drill a cross in, desperate Cardiff legs managing to divert it away.

Heaton was also well-placed to hold a Skrtel volley after the Slovakian popped up in the area from another corner.

With tiredness visibly setting in, the pace dropped slightly. The change in tempo didn't lead to a change in the pattern of the action. Still it was Liverpool pressing and Cardiff soaking up the danger.

Downing, having moved to the right flank, then cut inside and hit a deflected effort which Heaton pushed out.

Cardiff, with Peter Whittingham's clever passing at their core, continued to be efficient with the possession that came their way and nearly won it late on. A quick free-kick eventually led to Miller shooting just over the top. The look on the number nine's face illustrated how close he had been.

That was the last of the normal time action. Extra-time brought more of what had gone before.

Suarez shot low only for Heaton to once more save. From the resulting corner, the number seven's header was blocked on the line.

Tension in the stands was accompanied by cramp on the pitch. Bellamy, Downing and Johnson all went close to no avail.

At the halfway point of the additional 30 minutes, You'll Never Walk Alone bellowed out from the red masses.

Kuyt, one of their favourites, entered the action from the bench and was soon celebrating in from of them.

The Dutchman's attempt at a cross was diverted away from the six-yard box. When it came back to him he instantly returned it towards goal and beyond Heaton to make it 2-1.

Cardiff refused to relent and forced a series of corners as the clock edged towards 120 minutes. Kuyt managed to clear one from under his own bar, but there was nothing he could do at the next set-piece.

He and Turner challenged for possession almost on the line, and it was the Cardiff man who managed to divert it in to set up the penalty shoot-out.

In a pulse-quickening beginning to the spot-kicks, Heaton saved excellently from Gerrard before Miller hit the post.

Then Adam struck his effort wide and Cardiff went one up through Cowie.

Kuyt cancelled that out and Rudy Gestede then missed to leave it 1-1 after three attempts each.

Man of the match Downing was the next to succeed, but Whittingham matched him to raise the tension levels even higher.

Johnson was Liverpool's fifth taker. He converted, meaning Anthony Gerrard had to do the same. He didn't and our first honour since 2006 was secured.

Dalglish has now become only the third manager to win all three major trophies in English football. More importantly, it guarantees European football for next season.

JH

LIVERPOOL (4-2-3-1): Reina, Johnson, Skrtel, Agger (Carragher 86), Enrique, Gerrard, Adam, Downing, Henderson (Bellamy 58) Carroll (Kuyt 103), Suarez. Subs not used: Doni, Maxi, Spearing, Kelly.

CARDIFF (4-2-3-1): Heaton, McNaughton (Blake 106), Hudson (Gerrard 99), Taylor, Turner (Kiss 90), Cowie, Whittingham, Gunnarsson, Gestede, Mason, Miller. Subs not used: Marshall, Earnshaw, Conway, Naylor.

REFEREE: Mark Clattenburg
BOOKED: Henderson (52, foul)
ATTENDANCE: 89,041
MAN OF THE MATCH: Downing

CHARLIE ADAM:
7 After Steven Gerrard's corner is cleared, Adam takes one from right side and is jeered by Cardiff supporters following his goal for Blackpool in the play-off final two seasons ago. The corner is good, finding Martin Skrtel at the back post, but his header goes straight into the hands of goalkeeper Tom Heaton.

9 Passes ball back to Reina in deep midfield.

10 Closes down Peter Whittingham and forces the midfielder into surrendering possession.

14 Gains possession in midfield and feeds Glen Johnson who gives the ball back. He then finds Stewart Downing who has drifted infield.

15 Becomes deepest player in the team and takes the ball off Pepe Reina. Eventually he retains the ball and crosses for Andy Carroll who heads over.

18 Wins the ball back from Kenny Miller before finding Jose Enrique free on the left of the defence.

22 With a swoosh of a left foot, finds Luis Suarez in space.

32 Jordan Henderson's run results in half clearance from Ben Turner. The ball falls to Adam who fires wide from 25 yards.

43 Carries the ball 30 yards but upended by Kevin McNaughton

48 A cross-field pass finds Andy Carroll.

51 From a free-kick, Daniel Agger connects but Turner manages to head over.

52 A fierce shot is deflected over by Turner again.

72 Retrieves possession from Johnson and gives it wide to Gerrard who finds Johnson again before a corner is surrendered.

76 Tackles ex Rangers team-mate Miller in dangerous area and calms play by passing back to Pepe Reina.

85 A fine shot forces Heaton into a parry.

EXTRA-TIME

104 Wins possession and finds Bellamy but his shot ends up over the bar.

Carling Cup
WINNERS

'WORDS CAN'T DESCRIBE IT. IT'S FANTASTIC – IT'S WHAT THE LADS HAVE WORKED SO HARD FOR AND I THINK WE DESERVED IT. WE DIDN'T PLAY GREAT THROUGHOUT THE GAME BUT I THINK THERE WAS ONLY GOING TO BE ONE WINNER.'

GLEN JOHNSON:

"Words can't describe it. It's fantastic – it's what the lads have worked so hard for and I think we deserved it. We didn't play great throughout the game but I think there was only going to be one winner.

"We're very grateful for the fans' support and I hope they enjoyed it. The lads were cramping up there towards the end and when you hear them chanting, that's what gives you the extra little bit to push on.

"With my penalty, I just tried to blank out as much as possible and it was just me against the keeper. So I tried to get my head down and just put it in the net – that's all."

DIRK KUYT:

"We never stopped believing and that is why we have won the trophy. Even when Steven missed his penalty, I said to him we would still get back into it as there were a number of penalties to be taken.

"I knew when it came to my penalty that I had to score. I had cleared off the line 30 seconds from the end as well and scored in extra-time, so it was a good afternoon for me and for the team.

"The most important thing in football is belief and we showed today we have that in the squad. It's a great day for us."

'I KNEW WHEN IT CAME TO MY PENALTY THAT I HAD TO SCORE. I HAD CLEARED OFF THE LINE 30 SECONDS FROM THE END AS WELL AND SCORED IN EXTRA-TIME, SO IT WAS A GOOD AFTERNOON FOR ME AND FOR THE TEAM.'

'WE KNEW IT WAS GOING TO BE DIFFICULT. FINALS ALWAYS ARE. WE THOUGHT WE'D WON IT THEN THEY FOUGHT BACK AND WERE OUTSTANDING ALL THE WAY THROUGH. I DO FEEL SORRY FOR THEM BUT I'M DELIGHTED FOR US.'

CRAIG BELLAMY:

"Kuyt scored a fantastic goal and the game needed that. Then he scored a penalty in the shoot-out as well and it shows you the character he has. He gave us a big lift.

"He told us to keep believing and continue with our normal approach.

"We knew it was going to be difficult. Finals always are. We thought we'd won it then they fought back and were outstanding all the way through. I do feel sorry for them but I'm delighted for us.

"We'll have to wait and see what the future holds. As players we certainly don't think it's the end of the season. Yes, we have a trophy but we need to keep working hard if we want to be at the levels we really want to be at; where this club deserves to be."

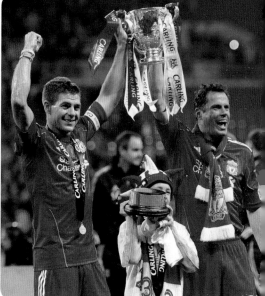

JORDAN HENDERSON:

"It was a roller-coaster but we're overjoyed. It was a great feeling at the end when we won.

"All the players and the manager and backroom staff have wanted to win it from day one. This can give us massive confidence to go on and win more things. For me personally, it makes me want to work harder and kick on.

"You could see the togetherness in the lads. Even when it went to 2-2, we went and tried to get the third.

"Cardiff were brilliant today. I feel sorry for them a little bit. But this can be a platform for us and hopefully there will be more to come."

'WE ALL THE PLAYERS AND THE MANAGER AND BACKROOM STAFF HAVE WANTED TO WIN IT FROM DAY ONE. THIS CAN GIVE US MASSIVE CONFIDENCE TO GO ON AND WIN MORE THINGS. FOR ME PERSONALLY, IT MAKES ME WANT TO WORK HARDER AND KICK ON.'

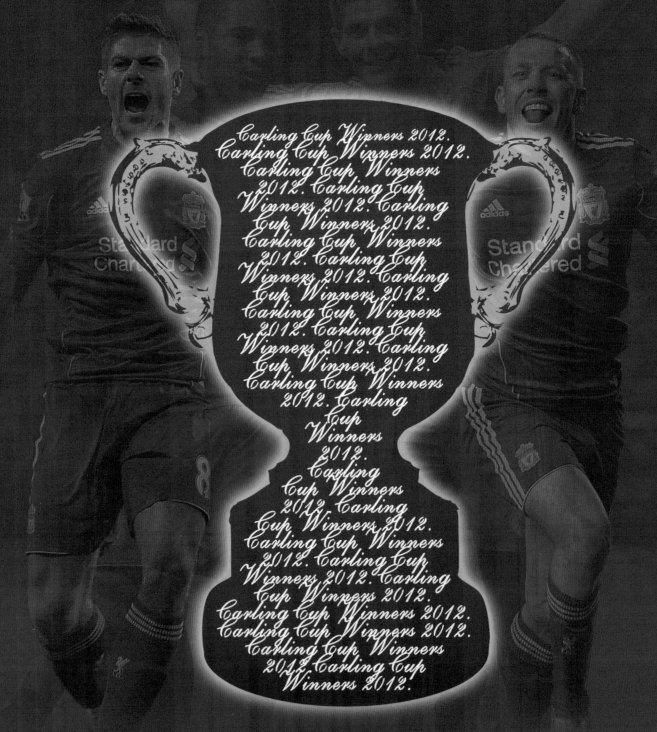

JOSE ENRIQUE:

"I didn't know this feeling before. It's amazing to win something like this. When Cardiff scored the second, if I'm honest I thought we might lose the game, so it's an amazing feeling – I can't explain it. It's the best feeling I ever had in football, for sure.

"If I had to take a penalty, I would take one - but, if I'm honest, I didn't want to because I'm no good at taking penalties!

"Like always the fans were amazing – that's no surprise. This is for them as well. They enjoy it like we do – maybe even more. It's amazing but now we have the league games and the FA Cup. I'll celebrate with my family and friends and I am really, really, really happy."

'I DIDN'T KNOW THIS FEELING BEFORE. IT'S AMAZING TO WIN SOMETHING LIKE THIS. WHEN CARDIFF SCORED THE SECOND, IF I'M HONEST I THOUGHT WE MIGHT LOSE THE GAME, SO IT'S AN AMAZING FEELING – I CAN'T EXPLAIN IT. IT'S THE BEST FEELING I EVER HAD IN FOOTBALL.'

Five of our best
League Cup final goals

FOLLOWING Dirk Kuyt's fine strike at Wembley, we look back at five of the Reds' best League Cup final goals...

KENNY DALGLISH
2-1, Vs WEST HAM (REPLAY), 01/04/81

Two weeks after the teams had played out a 1-1 draw at Wembley, they competed for the cup again at Villa Park.

John Lyall's second division side, FA Cup winners in 1980, were finally defeated thanks to goals from first Dalglish, and then Alan Hansen.

Dalglish's effort came after his clever run was found by Terry McDermott's chipped pass. On the stretch, the Scot managed to brilliantly angle a volley in to the net.

RONNIE WHELAN
2-1 Vs MAN UNITED (AET), 26/03/83

Alan Kennedy fed possession to the 21-year-old Irishman on the edge of the area before continuing his run forward.

Whelan attempted to work the ball back to him, only for the pass to be blocked. Without taking a touch the Dubliner readjusted his feet and, from the edge of the box, casually bent the ball into the far corner. "Brilliant goal," John Motson screamed.

STEVE MCMANAMAN
2-1, Vs BOLTON, 02/04/95

Steve McManaman bewitched Bolton with a couple of stunning solo goals as the Reds claimed a record fifth League Cup triumph.

The second was probably the better of the brace. Another successful solo slalom saw him ghost past Scott Green, Jason McAteer and Mark Seagraves before curling a low right foot shot beyond Keith Branagan.

ROBBIE FOWLER
1-1, Vs B'HAM (5-4 ON PENS), 25/02/01

Half an hour in against the Blues, Sander Westerveld sent a kick into the Birmingham half and Emile Heskey won a flick-on.

Robbie Fowler anticipated it perfectly and latched on to it to send a brilliant dipping volley past Ian Bennett. The skipper for the day would also score a penalty in the shoot-out win.

JOHN ARNE RIISE
2-3, Vs CHELSEA (AET), 27/02/05

To score any goal just 45 seconds into a final is memorable; the Norwegian did so with a cracking volley which flew past Petr Cech. Chelsea had kicked off before giving away possession. Fernando Morientes battled his way past a few defenders before clipping a cross to the back post, where the unmarked Riise superbly planted an outside of the foot volley into the net.

STEWART DOWNING:

"We made hard work of it. It was a tough game, we ran on empty a little bit at the end but credit to us it's a very good win at the end.

"Cardiff were very good. Credit to them, they've been brilliant all the way through the rounds. We knew it was going to be tough today, People expected us to turn up and win three or four-nil but that wasn't the case. Right to the end they were there and they were a little bit unlucky.

"I thought we'd won it when Dirk scored as they were a bit tired. But credit to them they never gave up all day, they kept going. It's a cruel way to lose on penalties but I thought we were the better team.

"(When Stevie and Charlie missed) I thought 'Maybe it's not going to be our day. You're thinking: "If those two are missing what's going to happen? But credit to the lads we kept going – we've got a great goalkeeper in Pepe, who has a good presence and in the end we got the job done."

'WE MADE HARD WORK OF IT. IT WAS A TOUGH GAME, WE RAN ON EMPTY A LITTLE BIT AT THE END BUT CREDIT TO US IT'S A VERY GOOD WIN AT THE END'

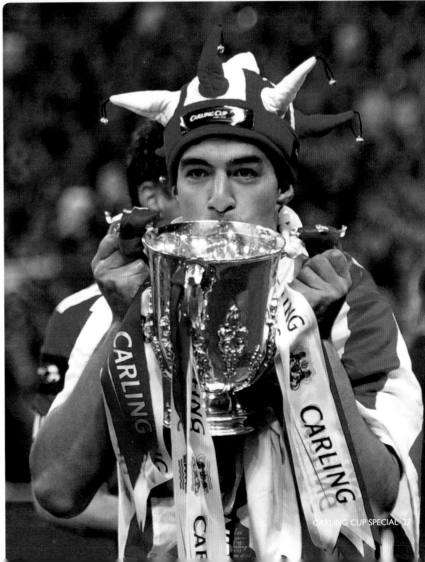

'IT'S A GOOD START AND IT WOULD BE GREAT TO GO ON AND DO WELL IN THE FA CUP AS WELL, BUT WE WON'T BE TAKING ANYTHING FOR GRANTED. AT LIVERPOOL WE WANT TO BE IN EUROPE EVERY YEAR, SO IT'S NICE TO HAVE IT ALREADY IN THE BAG'

JAMIE CARRAGHER:

"I can't think of us ever having an easy final. I always thought it was going to be a difficult game anyway. There wasn't going to be many goals in it. When there's a game of this importance at Wembley, it's always going to be like this.

"It's a good start and it would be great to go on and do well in the FA Cup as well, but we won't be taking anything for granted. At Liverpool we want to be in Europe every year, so it's nice to have it already in the bag.

"We've got two more targets and that includes the top four [in the Premier League]. But we want to be back here again.

"It means a lot to me and I'm sure he's the same. Everybody wants to see the club do well and make the supporters happy. I'm sure he's delighted but he's keeping a lid on it because there's a long way to go in the season yet."

MARTIN SKRTEL:

"It was a great game in a beautiful stadium with an unbelievable atmosphere.

 "I think we deserved it. It wasn't easy because they equalised with two minutes to go, but we just tried to keep our heads up and we got it on penalties.

 "I think everyone plays football for the trophies. This is the first one and I hope there will be more and more."

'IT WAS A GREAT GAME IN A BEAUTIFUL STADIUM WITH AN UNBELIEVABLE ATMOSPHERE. I THINK EVERYONE PLAYS FOOTBALL FOR THE TROPHIES. THIS IS THE FIRST ONE AND I HOPE THERE WILL BE MORE AND MORE.'

*'WE STUCK TOGETHER
AND KEPT ON BELIEVING.
WE HAVE PLAYERS IN THE
SQUAD THAT HAVE BEEN
IN THAT SITUATION A FEW
TIMES BEFORE'*

DANIEL AGGER:

"It doesn't really matter [that the game finished on penalties]. We won and everybody is very proud to be able to say that. This is what we work for every single day.

"We stuck together and kept on believing. We have players in the squad that have been in that situation a few times before.

"It is always sweet when you win a final and a medal, no matter what the circumstances are. We knew that if we just continued creating chances, we'd eventually get through and that happened.

"We always knew that. Every single game is important. There is so much to win with so many good games to look forward to."

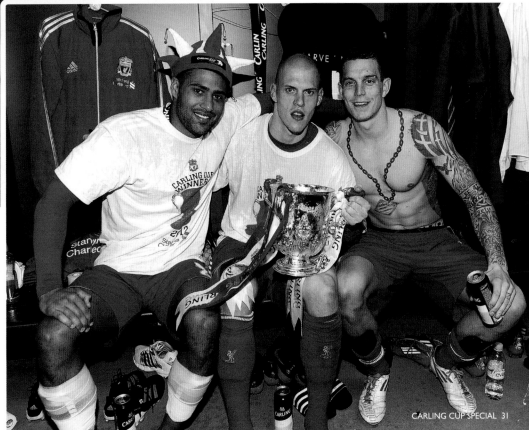

LIVERPOOL FC AT WEMBLEY

YEAR	OPPONENTS	COMPETITION	RESULT	SCORERS
1950	Arsenal	FA Cup Final	Lost 0-2	-
1965	Leeds	FA Cup Final	Won 2-1	Hunt, St John
1971	Arsenal	FA Cup Final	Lost 1-2	Heighway
1974	Newcastle	FA Cup Final	Won 3-0	Keegan 2, Heighway
1974	Leeds	FA Charity Shield	Won 1-1	Boersma
				(Liverpool won 6-5 on penalties)
1976	Southampton	FA Charity Shield	Won 1-0	Toshack
1977	Manchester Utd	FA Cup Final	Lost 1-2	Case
1977	Manchester Utd	FA Charity Shield	Drew 0-0	-
1978	Nottingham Forest	League Cup Final	Drew 0-0	-
1978	FC Bruges	European Cup Final	Won 1-0	Dalglish
1979	Arsenal	FA Charity Shield	Won 3-1	McDermott 2, Dalglish
1980	West Ham United	FA Charity Shield	Won 1-0	McDermott
1981	West Ham United	League Cup Final	Drew 1-1	A. Kennedy
1982	Tottenham Hotspur	League Cup Final	Won 3-1	Whelan 2, Rush
1982	Tottenham Hotspur	FA Charity Shield	Won 1-0	Rush
1983	Manchester United	League Cup Final	Won 2-1	A. Kennedy, Whelan
1983	Manchester United	FA Charity Shield	Lost 0-2	-
1984	Everton	League Cup Final	Drew 0-0	-
1984	Everton	FA Charity Shield	Lost 0-1	-
1986	Everton	FA Cup Final	Won 3-1	Rush 2, Johnston
1986	Everton	FA Charity Shield	Drew 1-1	Rush
1987	Arsenal	League Cup Final	Lost 1-2	Rush
1988	Wimbledon	FA Cup Final	Lost 0-1	-
1988	Wimbledon	FA Charity Shield	Won 2-1	Aldridge 2
1989	Everton	FA Cup Final	Won 3-2	Aldridge, Rush 2
1989	Arsenal	FA Charity Shield	Won 1-0	Beardsley
1990	Manchester United	FA Charity Shield	Drew 1-1	Barnes
1992	Sunderland	FA Cup Final	Won 2-0	Thomas, Rush
1992	Leeds United	FA Charity Shield	Lost 3-4	Rush, Saunders, Strachan o.g.
1995	Bolton Wanderers	League Cup Final	Won 2-1	McManaman 2
1996	Manchester United	FA Cup Final	Lost 0-1	-
2012	Cardiff City	League Cup Final	Won 2-2	Skrtel, Kuyt
				(Liverpool won 3-2 on penalties)

LIVERPOOL SCORERS AT WEMBLEY

Ian Rush	10
John Aldridge	3
Terry McDermott	3
Ronnie Whelan	3
Kenny Dalglish	2
Steve Heighway	2
Kevin Keegan	2
Alan Kennedy	2
Steve McManaman	2
John Barnes	1
Peter Beardsley	1
Phil Boersma	1
Jimmy Case	1
Roger Hunt	1
Craig Johnston	1
Dirk Kuyt	1
Dean Saunders	1
Martin Skrtel	1
Ian St John	1
Michael Thomas	1
John Toshack	1
own goal	1

RECORD LEAGUE CUP APPEARANCES

Ian Rush	78
Bruce Grobbelaar	70
Alan Hansen	68
Phil Neal	66
Kenny Dalglish	59
Ray Clemence	55
Mark Lawrenson	50
Ronnie Whelan	50
Emlyn Hughes	46
Alan Kennedy	45
Graeme Souness	45
Phil Thompson	43
Ian Callaghan	42
Steve Nicol	42
Sammy Lee	39
Steve Heighway	38
Terry McDermott	36
Robbie Fowler	35
Craig Johnston	35
Ray Kennedy	35

RECORD LEAGUE CUP SCORERS

Ian Rush	48
Robbie Fowler	29
Kenny Dalglish	27
Ronnie Whelan	14
Steve McMahon	13
Danny Murphy	11
David Fairclough	10
Steve McManaman	10
Steven Gerrard	9
David Johnson	9
Jan Molby	9
Michael Owen	9
Graeme Souness	9

LIVERPOOL MANAGERS IN LEAGUE CUP

MANAGERS	PLD	WON	DRAWN	LOST	FOR	AGAINST	TROPHIES	FINALS LOST
Bill Shankly	30	13	9	8	51	35	0	0
Bob Paisley	53	32	13	8	98	31	3	1
Joe Fagan	16	8	7	1	27	9	1	0
Graeme Souness	16	7	6	3	38	22	0	0
Roy Evans	21	17	1	3	42	14	1	0
Evans/ Houllier	2	1	0	1	4	4	0	0
Gerard Houllier	18	13	0	5	50	24	2	0
Rafa Benitez	17	11	0	6	31	27	0	1
Roy Hodgson	1	0	0	1	2	2	0	0
Kenny Dalglish (both spells)	38	24	8	6	86	36	1	1
TOTAL	212	126	44	42	429	204	8	3

Compiled by Ged Rea & Dave Ball

Various Liverpool FC supporters at the Carling Cup Final 2012, Wembley Stadium. Scarves read "LIVERPOOL FC", "YOU'LL NEVER WALK ALONE", "KING KENNY". Signs include "DON'T BUY THE Sun", "THE TRUTH 96 DEAD". A banner reads "DISTANCE IS NOT FOR THE FEAR, IT IS FOR THE BOLD, FROM INDON... TO PLEDGE OUR SUPPORT, TO SH... THE WORLD WE STAND BY THE BIGREDS". A handmade sign reads "THE ANFIELD CAT IS ERE".

A closer look at the impact four players made in our League Cup history – and what they're doing now

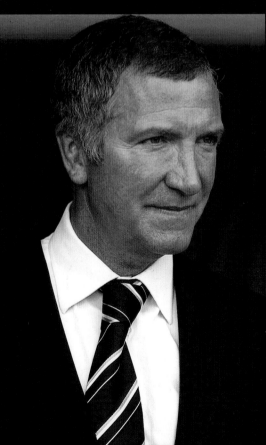

GRAEME SOUNESS

WHAT HE DID...

THE steely Scottish midfielder captained Liverpool to three consecutive League Cup victories in the early 1980s.

His highlight came in 1984 when his fine long-range strike proved decisive.

Having drawn 0-0 with Everton in the first all-Merseyside final at Wembley, Souness' stunning drive proved enough to win the replay at Manchester City's Maine Road.

It capped a hard night's work as he and Craig Johnston battled for supremacy in the centre of the pitch with Everton duo Peter Reid and Kevin Richardson.

Souness recalled: "It was a great occasion for the city of Liverpool to have two teams in the final. It meant a lot to people. We were very lucky to come away from the first game with a draw; there were some harsh words exchanged at half-time, Alan Hansen cleared one off the line and there was some debate about it being handball.

"The replay was dour but memorable for me as I scored. I mis-controlled it and had my back to goal but flashed a leg at it and it just dipped in front of Everton keeper Neville Southall before going in."

WHAT HE DOES NOW...

THE 1983/84 season would be Souness' last at Anfield. After lifting the European Cup in Rome that May, he left Liverpool to try his luck in Italy with Sampdoria. Following a two-year spell abroad, he returned to Scotland to move into management with Rangers.

He later returned to Liverpool as manager in 1991, staying three years before embarking on spells in charge of Galatasaray, Southampton, Torino, Benfica, Blackburn and Newcastle.

He has been out of management since February 2006 but has carved out a career as a respected pundit on Sky Sports' Champions League coverage.

1981-1984

RONNIE WHELAN

WHAT HE DID...

WHELAN'S exploits in this competition earned him the nickname 'the Milk Cup kid'. A cheesy moniker it may have been, yet it was understandable given the youngster's impact in two successive Wembley finals.

Defeat had looked certain in the first of those. Spurs led through Steve Archibald's early strike and looked like adding the cup to the FA Cup they had secured in 1981, and would retain a few weeks later.

Then Whelan latched on to a David Johnson cross to place a low shot beyond former Anfielder Ray Clemence and set up extra-time. At the same end he also manoeuvred the ball over Clemence to collect a brace on his Wembley debut, before Ian Rush made it 3-1.

The following year it was Manchester United - the team where he had been on trial as a kid - on the receiving end. Again extra-time was required and Whelan popped up to bend a beautiful winner past Gary Bailey from the edge of the area.

In 1984 he didn't get on the scoresheet during the two games with Everton. But the number five played every minute of the absorbing all-Merseyside contest as we claimed the trophy for the fourth time in a row.

WHAT HE DOES NOW...

WHEN his 14-year spell at Anfield ended Whelan moved on to Southend United to become their player-manager. Spells in charge of Panionios (Greece) and Apollon Limassol and Olympiakos Nicosia of Cyprus followed before he became a pundit.

Nowadays he works for LFCTV and RTE in Ireland. Last year he released his autobiography 'Walk On My Life In Red'.

1982-1984

LEAGUE CUP HEROES

SANDER WESTERVELD

SIGNED by Gerard Houllier in the summer of '99 to be his first-choice goalkeeper, Sander Westerveld was the hero of the first ever penalty shoot-out in a major domestic cup final in English football.

The Dutch international keeper was popular with Kopites – "he's big, he's Dutch, we like him very much, Westerveld, Westerveld," – and his best moment in a Liverpool shirt came in the 2001 Worthington Cup final success against Birmingham City in Cardiff's Millennium Stadium.

A last-minute Darren Purse penalty had cancelled out Robbie Fowler's opener to take the game to extra-time and the League Cup final witnessed its first penalty shoot-out.

Westerveld saved Birmingham's first kick, from Simon Grainger, but Didi Hamann also missed to send the shoot-out into sudden death where the Reds' keeper pushed out Andy Johnson's penalty to secure a first piece of silverware since 1995 and leave Brum boss Trevor Francis in tears.

With 61 appearances that season, nobody appeared more often than Westerveld in Liverpool's historic treble-winning campaign, but after a glaring error at Bolton just three games into 2001/02 he was bombed out of the team after Jerzy Dudek and Chris Kirkland were signed by Houllier on the same day.

WHAT HE DOES NOW...

SOLD to Real Sociedad in December 2001 at the age of 27, Westerveld has had a somewhat nomadic career ever since.

He spent three seasons in San Sebastian, the last of which included a loan spell at Mallorca, before being signed by Portsmouth boss Alain Perrin in the summer of 2005. But he made just six appearances for Pompey before being sent to Everton for a two-game loan spell later that season and then returning to Spain for a year at Almeria.

Westerveld spent 2007/08 at Sparta Rotterdam, moved to Italian minnows AC Monza Brianza in 2009 and since October 2011 the 37-year-old has been the first choice keeper at South African side Ajax Cape Town, where his recent form has earned him media praise.

2001

STEVE MCMANAMAN

1995

IT is easy to forget that Steve McManaman was an FA Cup winner, aged just 20. By the time his goals helped Liverpool to victory in a League Cup final three years after, he already appreciated what it was like to prepare, perform and succeed at one of English football's showpiece occasions.

The winger, who became the central pivot of all Liverpool's creative play, conjured two moments of individual excellence to defeat Bolton Wanderers in April 1995.

His opener came from a pass by John Barnes; receiving the ball in central midfield, he evaded the attentions of Dutchman Richard Sneekes before drifting wide further. Afraid to make a challenge, Scott Green let him pass before McManaman side-footed underneath Keith Branagan.

"People say it was a great goal because of the distance I carried it," McManaman recalls. "But the finish was a bit of a disappointment. The goalkeeper should probably have saved it."

There was no doubt about his second. From Jamie Redknapp's cross-field sweep, McManaman gained control on the left. Again he teased right-back Green, accelerating past him, then Alan Stubbs. This time, Branagan was well beaten.

"It was an unusually warm day at Wembley and I think we were the fitter side. It probably gave me the bit of space I needed," McManaman added.

WHAT HE DOES NOW...

McMANAMAN retired as a player in 2005 after a highly successful spell at Real Madrid before moving to Manchester City.

He has since worked in the media for a number of television stations as well as helping advise the principal owner of Birmingham City. He is still open to a career as a football manager.

"I took my first coaching badge last year [2008] in case I fancied it in the future," he said. "Ten or 15 years ago, it would have been attractive to an ex-footballer like me, but now management is a very difficult job to hold down. There is also a dearth of young English managers – good managers like Alan Curbishley and Gareth Southgate who want to get in at the right club – but can't. Maybe in time, I'll feel differently."

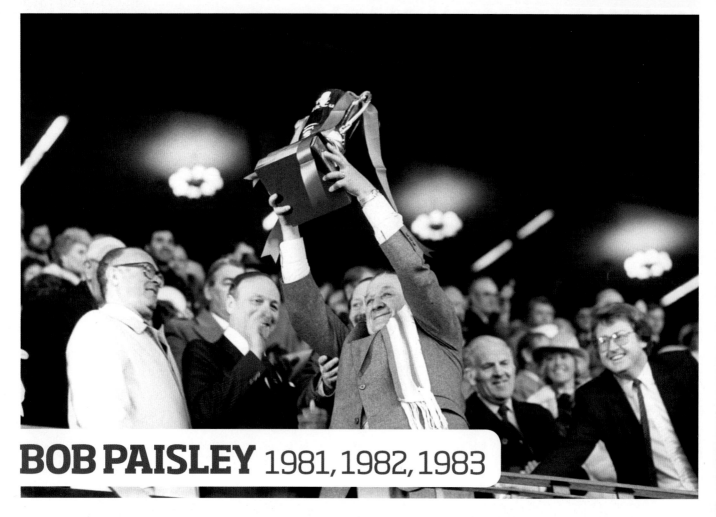

BOB PAISLEY 1981, 1982, 1983

ALTHOUGH Bob Paisley led Liverpool to more League Cup titles than any other manager, Kenny Dalglish has the best statistical record than any other boss in terms of victories and goals scored.

Dalglish, whose first League Cup winners medal came with the victory over Cardiff City, had previously lost one final to Arsenal in 1987. En route to Wembley that year, the Reds beat Fulham in the second round first leg 10-0, thus enhancing Dalglish's overall record.

Before Cardiff, Dalglish had managed Liverpool in 37 League Cup matches, winning 24, drawing seven and losing six. During that time, his sides had scored 84 goals, conceding 34.

By comparison Bob Paisley, the first Liverpool manager to win the League Cup before making the competition staple fodder season after season at the beginning of the 1980s, took charge of 53 matches, winning 32, drawing 13 and losing eight. Under

his stewardship Liverpool scored 98 times, conceding 31. In four finals, they won three times, losing once.

Gerard Houllier also holds an impressive record. Between 1999 and 2004, he managed 18 games, winning 13, losing five. Due to the knock-out format of the League Cup by then, he never drew a match. In winning the trophy on two occasions, Liverpool scored 50 goals and let in 24.

Joe Fagan lost the least number of League Cup games as Liverpool boss. During a two-year spell in charge, he lost just once, to Tottenham Hotspur at White Hart Lane in October 1984. In total, he won eight of 16 games, drawing seven, scoring 27 and letting in just nine.

Bill Shankly, meanwhile, won 13 of his 30 games, drawing nine and losing eight. His teams scored 51 goals, conceding 35.

JOE FAGAN
1984

GERARD
HOULLIER 2001, 2003

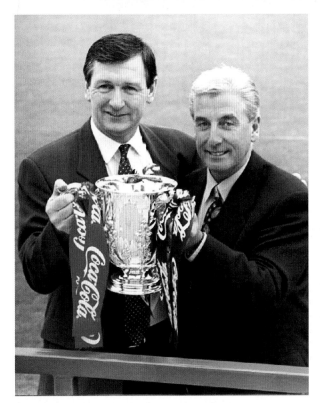

ROY EVANS
1995

AWAYDAYS
EXETER

AWAY WE GO TO WEMBLEY

From Arsenal's Emirates to Exeter's St James' Park, a week of contrasts saw one important thing in common - two Reds wins. **CHRIS MCLOUGHLIN** followed the fans as they began a series of road trips on the way to Wembley

THEY say you can't go anywhere without meeting a Scouser. Exeter is no different.

Liverpool were in town so there were always going to be Scousers about, but the odds of meeting a lad you last saw at school 17 years ago stood in the station must've been about the same as it was for Kenny to play up front.

There, stood in Exeter St David's station, was a lad called Dave who I'd not seen since 1994, despite us both being regular away travellers. I wouldn't have recognised him if he didn't still have his school uniform on...

Like quite a few others at St David's, he was down in Devon for the game – and the day trip that goes with it.

With no European aways to look forward to this year, the Carling Cup has gained extra prominence, not just for Liverpool

second round game since 1999 as a 'must make' with an overnight stay thrown in for good measure.

At the same time, there was a sense of trepidation about the game. Having been embarrassed by League Two Northampton at Anfield last season, a repeat performance against League One Exeter was the last thing we needed.

If we were to beat the Grecians, we'd have to earn it.

My journey down from Liverpool, via Birmingham (not very) New Street is uneventful, but long. You know you've been on a train for a while when the bloke pushing the buffet trolley has grown a beard by the time he comes back past you.

By the time we get to Bristol Temple

12. I've no idea how it got its name, but if you're ever going down there it's next door to number 10.

Just down the road, not far from the station, is The Imperial, a Wetherspoons pub that is so big they show classic movies in their garden cinema.

It looks as good a place as any to get some pre-match scran and as soon as I get in a bloke with 'Adelphi' on his t-shirt walks past.

Moments later, before I can say 'just cook will yer' the barman informs me he is a student in Liverpool and it has "weirded him out" hearing so many Scousers today. Looks like I'm not the only Red in here.

I get chatting to a couple of lads in the beer garden who are hoping to see a strong Liverpool team, a good win and no rain. Two outta three ain't bad, as a famous Hartlepool fan once sung.

Exeter is a historic town with its cathedral, quirky side-street shops and university drawing a mixture of tourists and students to it. You'll also find a club with a very famous name.

By 4pm the queue for The Cavern is already snaking down a narrow paved street.

'There aren't too many clubs you can play further down south than Exeter City – it's quicker to fly to Istanbul than get the train there '

but also for Kopites. A trip to Exeter City for the first time since 1981 was an appealing prospect for away day regulars, particularly those who wanted to tick a new ground off on their 'to visit' list.

There aren't too many clubs you can play further down south than Exeter City – it's quicker to fly to Istanbul than get the train there – so a lot of travelling Kopites looked at our first League Cup

Meads, Noel Gallagher is warbling out 'Half the World Away' on my iPod. "This old town don't smell too pretty," he sings. No wonder so many people get on the train here.

After four-and-a-half hours I'm finally in Exeter and, after exchanging pleasantries with my former school mate, off I go to find the B&B I'm getting me head down in for the night – Number

THE SIGHTS OF EXETER: Even hundreds of miles away you can always find a few Scousers

Ginger's The Wildhearts may not quite be up there with John Lennon's The Beatles, but it looks like they'll be playing to a decent crowd tonight. So too will Exeter – St James' Park is a 8,290 sell-out.

Exeter town centre doesn't just have a link to Liverpool's past. Next to The Cavern stands Boston Tea Party, a tea-shop frequented by thirsty tourists, hungry office workers and Earl greying pensioners.

It may be named after our owners' home city, but travelling Kopites are conspicuous by their absence. They're here for the Carling, not a cuppa, and there are other places to be.

While some Exeter and Liverpool fans swap stories as they mingle in the Duke of York, Bowling Green and Sorry Head pubs close to St James'

WELCOME TO ST JAMES PARK

Park, others head up to the ground early. The contrast to your typical Premier League grounds is stark.

Situated on St James' Road, the home fans – 'we are Exeter, say we are Exeter' – congregate on the Big Bank behind one of the goals.

To their left is the new-ish Flybe Stand, home of executive boxes and the club shop, and to the right is the rickety old Stagecoach Grandstand with wooden floors and an old fashioned glass-fronted press box at the back.

That just leaves St James' Road terrace – aka the away end – and a terrace on St James' Road pretty much sums it up. If it wasn't for a corrugated iron fence, Liverpool's fans would be stood in the road.

Not since the FA Cup trip to Yeovil in 2004 have the travelling Kop stood on terracing for a game and with no roof above them, they were well and truly open to the elements. Or the weather, as the elements are also known.

In truth, the prospect of getting such a rudimentary space was something many Reds were buzzing about. Old-school away days are few and far between now, while standing up at a Liverpool match is an even rarer occurrence, so the novelty of doing so at Exeter was a cause of 1980s-style excitement.

An early chant of 'we pay your benefits' from the Exeter fans and the travelling Kop's 'Maggie Thatcher' banner make it feel

like it really is the '80s again. All that was missing were the perms and 'taches.

Having been at The Emirates for a Premier League game four days earlier, Exeter is quite a different experience for Liverpool's players on first arrival.

At Arsenal, Liverpool's Ellison's team bus is waved through to a road underneath the stadium where the

OLD SCHOOL: A step back in time to visit an old fashioned ground like St James' Park was something many fans relished

players alight in privacy. At Exeter they get off in the street and go into the ground through a big red gate behind the away terracing, prompting a couple of hundred fans to line the sides of St James' Road to grab a glimpse of their heroes.

The biggest cheers are reserved for Kenny, Jamie Carragher, Luis Suarez, Andy Carroll, Pepe Reina and Dirk Kuyt, although as kitman Graham Carter also gets cheered you can tell most Reds are in a boisterous mood.

To reach my press-box seat in the Stagecoach Family Stand, I have to walk around half the pitch in front of a packed away end. Walking towards me the other way is a familiar face.

"Alright lad, yer ok?" Jamie Carragher is on his way down to the away end to sign autographs for kids and pose for a few pictures. Such gestures can be remembered for a lifetime and Carra never loses sight of that.

He is one of the eight players Kenny has left out from the side that started against Arsenal, but the team he puts on the pitch is still strong. The fact that skipper for the night Pepe Reina gets his first start in the Carling Cup since the 4-3 win against Reading in 2006 is a signal of Kenny's intent. It may be August, but he's already plotting a route back to Wembley.

The line-up delights supporters of both sides and as I take my seat, directly in front of Reds legend Jimmy Case who is commentating for Radio Merseyside, and with a giant 'Stansfield 9' shirt unfurled on the Big Bank in tribute to the former Exeter striker Adam Stansfield who tragically died of colorectal cancer aged just 31, I fancy us to win well.

And we do. Suarez is at his mesmerising best. Jay Spearing charges around the midfield like a Tasmanian devil. Charlie Adam's corners are unpredictable and difficult to deal with. Jordan Henderson is a pacy threat down the right. The kids at the back – Danny Wilson, Jon Flanagan and Jack Robinson – look composed and assured. We've plainly got strength in depth again.

An early collar-bone injury to Raul Meireles – which turns out to be his last act in a Liverpool shirt before defecting to Chelsea – after a crunching challenge forces him off, but as soon as Suarez opens the scoring in front of the travelling Kopites behind the goal you never really feel like an upset is on the cards.

Quite how good a view of the goal the lads stood on garden walls and rooves behind the stand get I don't know, but it must be decent given the game is on Sky.

It was shortly after the first goal when it starts to drizzle. And then the rain gets a

»

'At the Emirates Arsenal fans who were getting wet left their seats. Our fans are made of sterner stuff'

bit harder. And more sustained.

On Saturday, down at The Emirates, the same thing had happened. When it did, most of the first five rows or so of the Arsenal fans, who were getting wet despite being sat in a multi-million pound new stadium with a roof over them, left their seats. Some stood at the back of the stands, some went home.

Liverpool supporters are made of sterner stuff.

Despite taking a soaking to almost rival Wimbledon 1994/95 when the Kop was being rebuilt ("We only sing when it's raining"), they don't move. Instead of getting off, they start bouncing. Instead of whinging, they start singing.

Even at half-time a chorus of 'Dirky Kuyt ole' rings out, as does the Lucas Leiva 'Love is in the Air' tune later on, even though the Brazilian isn't playing.

On the touchline, the Liverpool manager, fresh from a soaking at Arsenal, pulls his black manager's coat on over his suit. Exeter boss Paul Tisdale's coat has a designer feel to it, although the flat cap he dons is straight from the Alan Ball book of fashion.

Liverpool's second half goals could have come straight from Kenny himself.

Clinical strikes from Maxi and Andy Carroll, courtesy of Suarez assists, ensure the home side become Exiter as far as the Carling Cup is concerned. Liverpool are in the third round.

The Grecians get a consolation goal back from Daniel Nardiello, who nets from the penalty spot with 10 minutes to play after a foul by Martin Skrtel on his comeback game. It prompts a 'there's only one team in Devon' rallying cry from the Exeter faithful, but

Liverpool aren't about to let their lead go west.

Applause from all four sides of the ground greets the final whistle and in a nice touch from Exeter, the second song played over the PA system at full-time is You'll Never Walk Alone.

Afterwards, in the cramped media suite, Dalglish is surrounded by journalists as he speaks of how pleased he is with the performance and goals, how Liverpool will treat the Carling Cup with the respect it deserves and how happy he is to see youngsters like Wilson, Flanno and Robbo give good accounts of themselves.

A journalist sniffing around for a transfer story pipes up. "Harry Redknapp said he's seen Joe Cole and..." "Has he?" quips Dalglish to much amusement. "Good. We've nothing to say other than what comes out of our football club."

The journo scurries off to see if he'll have more luck getting blood from a stone.

With the rain still bucketing down, I splash my way into the Duke of York at full-time where a rousing version of Fields of Anfield Road is ringing out over a post-match pint.

The next morning, on the train back to Liverpool, four seasoned travelling Kopites who drink in The Holt, Kensington, and who were at Exeter back in '81 are discussing who they want Liverpool to draw next.

"The Toffees at home," is one suggestion, but "Brighton away" is a popular alternative.

"We went to their old stadium under Kenny so it'd be nice to go down and see the new one," reasons one of the lads who is sat beside me.

"Anyhow, it'd be another great little away trip and that's what we all want."

WET AND WINDY: The Reds overcame difficult conditions to win through

NOW ON TO BRIGHTON

Luis runs Exeter ragged

EXETER 1 LIVERPOOL 3 (Carling Cup 2nd round) ST JAMES' PARK, 24.08.11

LUIS Suarez scored one and created two more on his Carling Cup debut as the Reds comfortably beat Exeter 3-1 at a soggy St James' Park to give Kenny Dalglish his 200th win as Liverpool manager.

The Uruguayan striker started the season in fine form and he ran the League One side ragged. By the time he left the pitch, to applause from both the travelling Kop and Exeter fans, his statistics for 2011/12 read: played 3, goals 3, assists 3. Not bad for a player who hadn't completed 90 minutes by that point having only returned from the Copa America a few weeks earlier.

It was the first time the Reds have played in the second round of the competition since meeting Hull City in 1999/2000 and there was much speculation before the game about how strong a line-up Dalglish would field.

He made eight changes from the side that started against Arsenal, but such is the strength in depth Liverpool now have that it made little impact on how the Reds performed.

With Jay Spearing excellent in midfield, Charlie Adam keeping the ball moving quickly and the movement of Suarez, Maxi Rodriguez and Jordan Henderson causing problems, Liverpool forced a series of

corners early on with Martin Skrtel almost turning one into the net.

The loss of Meireles with a collarbone injury in the 20th minute saw Andy Carroll enter the fray and three minutes later the Reds were in front.

Adam, Spearing and Maxi combined to work the ball out to Henderson on the right and although Carroll couldn't get on the end of his cross, Suarez finished well.

The floodgates opened shortly afterwards, although unfortunately for the travelling Kopites on the uncovered terracing they opened in the sky rather than on the pitch.

With three young defenders in Danny Wilson, Jon Flanagan and Jack Robinson at the back alongside Skrtel, the Grecians may have fancied their chances of getting back into it, but all three showed why Dalglish rates them so highly. Wilson, in particular, looked composed in front of Reina, who was playing in his first League Cup game since 2006.

The only surprise was that it took Liverpool until the 55th minute to score again. This time Suarez turned creator. Played in down the right by Henderson, his first cross was blocked, but the Copa America winner found Maxi at the second attempt and he coolly side-footed into the net on his Carling Cup debut.

Three minutes later and the tie was over. Picking the ball up in a central area, Suarez nutmegged Troy Archibald-Henville and streaked forward before laying off to Carroll who, after taking a touch, smashed an unstoppable left-footed drive past Artur Krysiak from the edge of the box.

Nardiello pulled a goal back in the 80th minute from the penalty spot having been tripped by Skrtel in the box, but that couldn't take away from a professional performance by a Liverpool side that look intent on getting to Wembley.

EXETER (4-5-1): Krysiak, Golbourne, Jones, Coles (Nicholls 76), Duffy, Archibald-Henville, Noble, Shephard (McNish 65), Dunne, Nardiello, Bauza (Keohane 22). Subs not used: Pidgeley, Logan, Frear, Bennett.

LIVERPOOL (4-2-3-1): Reina, Flanagan, Robinson, Skrtel, Wilson, Spearing, Adam (Shelvey 77), Henderson, Maxi, Meireles (Carroll 20), Suarez (Downing 59). Subs not used: Doni, Jose Enrique, Kuyt, Carragher.
REFEREE: Tony Bates (Burslem)
BOOKED: Liverpool: Henderson (52, simulation)

1981

LIVERPOOL 1 WEST HAM 1 (AET)
WEST HAM 2 LIVERPOOL 1 (R)

AHEAD of the March final the Londoners were ten points clear at the top of the Second Division.

With just three minutes of extra-time left, despite appeals for offside, Alan Kennedy appeared to have won the tie for Liverpool when he converted a rebound.

However, Terry McDermott's habit of making headlines at Wembley continued as he handled a header from Bootle-born Alvin Martin on the line.

'The next morning I received a call from Peter Robinson, our chief executive, asking where the trophy was. I told him it was on the bus'

In the battle of the Rays, Stewart sent Clemence the wrong way from the penalty spot to earn a replay at Villa Park three weeks later when goals from Kenny Dalglish and Alan Hansen secured the League Cup for the first time.

Unfortunately, though, captain Phil Thompson mislaid the trophy on the way home. "Suffice to say a good night was had by all," the captain recalls. "The next morning I received a call from Peter Robinson, our chief executive, who asked where the trophy was.

"I told him it was on the bus. 'Yes I know,' he replied. 'I've just had a call from the depot in St Helens – the driver found it on the back seat when he was cleaning up! Don't let the next one out of your sight!'"

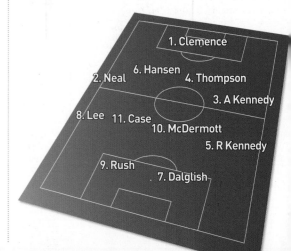

1. Clemence
6. Hansen
2. Neal
4. Thompson
3. A Kennedy
8. Lee   11. Case
10. McDermott
5. R Kennedy
9. Rush
7. Dalglish

1982

LIVERPOOL 3 TOTTENHAM 1 (AET)

MORE late drama ensued in another League Cup final decider.

Spurs, the FA Cup holders, led through Steve Archibald after 11 minutes. Only a goal-line clearance by Graeme Souness prevented Archibald doubling the advantage and that intervention proved crucial when Ronnie Whelan equalised three minutes from the end.

Before extra-time began Bob Paisley urged his men to stand up to show Spurs they weren't tired. Whether that tactic had an effect is unknown. What's

> 'I ran over the running track to celebrate. Only when I got there did I realise it was such a long way back'

certain is Liverpool were the better side in the additional period. Whelan again, and an Ian Rush effort ensured the cup was retained.

"It was my first trip to Wembley and a massive test," Whelan recalled. "Tottenham had a great side with players like Glenn Hoddle, Micky Hazard and Ossie Ardiles. They looked like they had the game won until I squeezed a shot past Ray Clemence towards the end and we got stronger in extra-time.

"I was so over the moon after getting my second that I ran over the running track to celebrate with our fans. Only when I got there did I realise it was such a long way back to the pitch and I was so tired that I barely made it."

1 Grobbelaar
4. Thompson
2. Neal   6. Lawrenson
                        3. A Kennedy
8. Lee   11. Souness
             10. McDermott
                        5. Whelan
9. Rush
       7. Dalglish

THE ROAD TO WEMBLEY

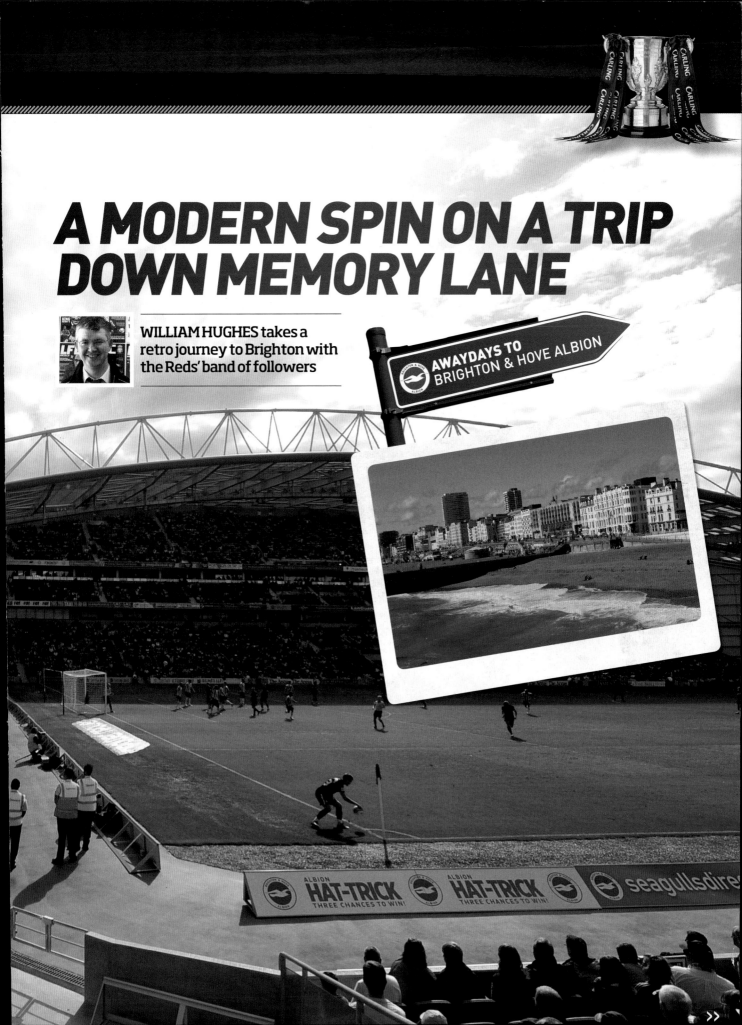

A MODERN SPIN ON A TRIP DOWN MEMORY LANE

WILLIAM HUGHES takes a retro journey to Brighton with the Reds' band of followers

AWAYDAYS TO
BRIGHTON & HOVE ALBION

ON the train back from Exeter, four seasoned travelling Kopites were discussing who they wanted to draw next in the Carling Cup.

Brighton away seemed a popular choice.

Phil Thompson, who had been on the St James' Park pitch throughout the Reds' 6-0 win in Devon in '81, must have agreed.

Three days later the former Reds captain joined Alan McInally on Sky Sports' Soccer Saturday show to conduct the third round draw.

Thommo, charged with drawing the home teams, picked out Brighton. 'Will play...,' added McInally, 'Liverpool'.

And so the scene was set for the Reds' first trip to Brighton's new 22,374-capacity Amex Stadium.

THERE is a retro feel about Liverpool Football Club these days. Not only is Kenny Dalglish back in the dugout but there is also a decidedly Eighties flavour to the make-up of English football's top-flight.

The return of teams such as QPR, Norwich and Swansea has helped add to that impression and so a cup tie with Brighton somehow felt right.

The Goldstone Ground, home to Brighton for five years shy of a century, was the scene of several cup clashes against Kenny's men during his previous spell in charge.

In fact, it was the venue for his last cup win of that era, a 3-2 FA Cup fourth round replay triumph secured courtesy of extra-time goals from Ian Rush and Steve McMahon.

During his playing days though, the boss was involved in a couple of FA Cup exits at the hands of the Seagulls.

In 1983, Liverpool went out in the fifth round at Anfield as Brighton, managed by Jimmy Melia and including Michael Robinson and match-winner Jimmy Case, registered a 2-1 win after Phil Neal had, for once, missed a penalty.

The following season Brighton also proved to be the Reds' undoing in a fourth round clash on the south coast with the back page of the Mirror screaming 'All Things Brighton Beautiful' as two goals in as many minutes from Gerry Ryan – also a scorer at Anfield the previous year – and Terry Connor sealed Liverpool's fate.

With all this talk of the Eighties, I half-expected to find a carriage full of lads with mullets and muzzies wearing skin-tight acid wash jeans passing round Rubik's cubes when I boarded the train at Lime Street on the morning of the game.

Instead carriage 'C' of the 9.48am Virgin Pendolino to London Euston was roughly divided 50/50 between sharp-suited business people and travelling Reds heading to the capital.

A table of four Liverpool fans sit opposite me. They made this part of the journey just three days earlier and saw pretty much everything that could go wrong do just that as Liverpool finished their game at Tottenham with nine men and a 4-0 reverse.

However, the Carling Cup has taken on a fresh significance for Liverpool this season with no European football to accommodate and the Kopite contingent are all looking forward to this 'new' away day and a first trip to Brighton's Amex Stadium.

The strength of the team fielded in the previous round at Exeter served to illustrate Dalglish's feelings on the matter. When it comes to any competition he's involved in, Liverpool are in it to win it.

As the train tilts its way towards Birmingham, conversation among the travelling Redmen turns to the likely team selection with at least two enforced changes to contemplate due to the one-match suspensions of Charlie Adam and Martin Skrtel.

"Stevie should be back and I think Danny Wilson and Coates will play," ventures one.

"I think we'll go with the two young lads at full-back, Flanagan and Robinson," offers another.

The journey takes just over two hours and as we pull in at Euston just after noon, the majority of the Liverpool fans decide to head into central London for lunch washed down with a pint or two.

I head for the underground to catch the 15-minute trip to Victoria, from where a further one-hour journey via East Croydon, Gatwick and Burgess Hill brings me to Brighton.

The sun is shining and the seagulls squawking as I head out of the station for the seafront hotel which will be home for the night.

It's a 10-minute walk down Queen's Road past familiar high street stores but also a Brighton and Hove Albion club shop, the Albion Kebab house, a Masonic Centre and the BBC Radio Sussex merchandise outlet.

In the lobby of the hotel - the UMI - is the familiar sound of Scouse accents.

"We've got quite a few of you in tonight!" says the young lad on reception. "You do know the team is staying just 100 yards down the road don't you?"

At first, I wonder whether my room has been daubed with grafitti. However, an explanatory note explains that each of the 77 rooms has been decorated with a quote.

This one reads: "Keep your eyes on the stars, and your feet on the ground."

It is attributed to former US president Theodore Roosevelt but could just as easily have been Bill Shankly.

After finding their own rooms, a dozen or so Reds take the almost obligatory walk along the pebbled beach to the pier.

The hazy afternoon sunshine is accompanied by a stiff sea breeze. It isn't replica shirt weather but despite being

Jimmy Case scores as Brighton beat the Reds at Anfield in 1983

an early Wednesday afternoon in late September, there is plenty going on.

It is not the pier head we are more familiar with and an amble along it reveals a 'mini-Blackpool' with amusement arcades, fun fair and other attractions such as the 'Big Air' bungee dive.

After taking in the sea air, it is time to head back into town in search of some pre-match grub.

The route takes in The Lanes, a quirky bohemian shopping venue hosting hundreds of independent retailers. On the way through, near which I bump into Radio Merseyside's Gary Flintoff and a couple of his colleagues. We agree that a sedate stroll through bustling Brighton is all part of one of the more pleasant away days the fixture list can offer.

In the Evening Star pub, a couple of minutes' walk from Brighton Railway Station on Surrey Street, dozens of Liverpool fans agree.

The benches outside are a sea of red and, inside, the compact bar area is full of scores more. There is a similar scene across the road at The Railway Bell.

The local ale, Harvey's, may have been brewed by humans but appears to be inspired by the divine. And all for three quid a pint.

I ask one fan for a prediction. '3-0 with Suarez scoring,' he suggests.

The bookmakers tend to agree with a Liverpool win. The local Ladbrokes are offering odds of 4-7 on a Reds success; the value is for Brighton fans willing to punt a tenner on a 2-1 win which would see a return of £170.

At a quarter to six it is time to take the 10-minute train ride to Falmer, the site of Brighton's new £93 million American Express Community Stadium or, more succinctly, the Amex.

Brighton supporters have had to endure turbulent times at the hands of unscrupulous owners during modern times.

In 1995 their former owners sold the Goldstone Ground to developers without arranging anything regarding a new home.

Inevitably protests followed but sadly the battle to save the crumbling Goldstone was lost. Brighton only survived because local businessman Dick Knight - saluted by a flag in the home end - seized control of the club. But Brighton were forced into a nomadic existence for more than a decade, sharing with Gillingham for two years before moving to the local athletics stadium - The Withdean - in 1999.

It was around that time that a site in Falmer was identified to build a new stadium. Yet though planning permission

was granted in 2002, opposition and appeals from the neighbouring Lewes council and local residents meant it was July 2007 before the club finally got the green light to build their new home.

Finally, after a decade-and-a-half of fears and frustrations, the Amex opened for business this season.

Gus Poyet's side – promoted as League One champions last term - have since built on that success, knocking Sunderland out of the Carling Cup in the previous round and going into their clash with the Reds in third place in The Championship.

When the team sheets arrive in the plush media lounge, the expected strong Liverpool side is in evidence with a full debut for Sebastian Coates, and a first full start in more than four years for Craig Bellamy. Steven Gerrard also returns to the squad, but starts on the bench.

There are also a couple of Liverpool links in the Brighton line-up.

Midfielder Alan Navarro came through the Reds' Academy before leaving for

Tranmere in 2002. Meanwhile winger Craig Noone - a committed Liverpool fan - admitted that he once looked down on Gerrard, but only because he was working on the skipper's house in his days working as a roofer while a young player at Skelmersdale United.

There is a good atmosphere inside the stadium and in the build-up to kick-off the fans trade chants of 'Seagulls, Seagulls' and 'Liverpool, Liverpool, Liverpool.' A cheerleading troupe, aka Gully's Girls, go through a routine on the pitch before the teams make their entrance to the Albion anthem Sussex By The Sea.

The bowl-like arena is an impressive sight and reminiscent of Huddersfield's Galpharm Stadium with its swooping arched rooves. The Liverpool fans - all 2,462 of them - are located in the freshly painted South Stand behind the goal.

By the end of the first 45 minutes, the paint on the goal at the opposite end was in need of a little sprucing up as Liverpool struck it three times.

Bellamy, the Redmen's star performer

>>

on the night, quashed fears of a White Hart Lane hangover with a seventh minute strike after being played in by Suarez. It is his first Liverpool goal since he netted at the Nou Camp in February 2007 and Dalglish punches the air in delight.

Bellamy, Suarez and Spearing all rattle the woodwork during the remainder of the half with the Welshman's 35-yard free-kick almost producing one of Liverpool's all-time best League Cup goals. 'A boiling strike,' as one Red puts it on the train back the following day.

With Maxi and Dirk Kuyt also combining well with Suarez and Bellamy, the Reds do a good job of silencing the expectant home crowd.

Ten minutes before half-time, Gerrard warms up for the first time and though it's in front of the Brighton fans, they break into spontaneous applause. As he acknowledges their warm reception, the away end belts out a couple of familiar chants in honour of their revered captain.

Somehow Liverpool's lead is only one-nil at the break and following a team talk from Gus Poyet, Brighton begin brightly after the re-start. Noone - later voted the sponsors' Brighton man of the match - becomes the fourth player of the night to hit the frame of the goal with a rasping 20-yard effort.

As Brighton tried to push forward in the final half-hour, a beach ball suddenly appeared among the home supporters. In case Seagulls fans had forgotten, Liverpool have been there and done that.

Thus far, Albion's stands have been unimaginatively named after the four points of the compass.

'We're North Stand, We're North Stand,' came a regular refrain from behind the home goal. 'We're West Stand, We're West Stand,' came the response from the side.

But with 10 minutes remaining Brighton's Carling Cup ambitions were going west.

Steven Gerrard had made his entrance to a rousing cheer in the 75th minute. After being out of action for six months, he needed just six minutes to make a contribution.

His clearance out of defence picked out the tireless Bellamy on the left flank. He showed good awareness to spot Maxi busting a gut to join him and found the Argentine with a pass back across the field.

He kept the move going by moving it

to his right, where the overlapping Kuyt arrived on cue to slide home his first goal of the season - again via the post.

It gave Liverpool a deserved two-goal cushion and was ample reward for Bellamy, who produce a phenomenal work rate at both ends of the pitch.

A 90th-minute penalty gave Brighton a consolation but a resolute Reds saw out the four added minutes to reach the fourth round.

As both sides were applauded from the pitch, Poyet warmly embraced his compatriots Suarez and Coates, just as he had done his former Chelsea team-mate Steve Clarke before kick-off.

But, all told, the Brighton boss could have no complaints about the outcome.

On the way out of the away end, you pass a gallery of favourites from Brighton and Hove Albion history.

One of those depicted, Jimmy Case, was interviewed at the side of the pitch

during the half-time interval as giant screens behind the goals showed footage of his 1983 goal at Anfield.

"I'm delighted that this stadium has been built for these fans," he says. "I know what they've been through standing in the wind and rain in their cagoules for years."

He is warmly applauded by both sets of fans and Reds will share his sentiments.

Liverpool fans enjoyed their trip and few would begrudge Brighton if they were to make the fixture a regular part of the top-flight calendar once again.

IT is quarter to eleven when the train chugs out of Falmer Station. Inside, the carriage is literally rocking with fans swaying while singing: "Oh when the Reds go marching in."

There are plenty of Brighton fans on board too and the banter bounces back and to.

On seeing a Liverpool fan who bears something of a passing resemblance to the Reds' number 18, the Albion supporters chant: 'Two Dirk Kuyts, there's only two Dirk Kuyts.' Both sets of fans have enjoyed the night.

At breakfast the next day, a handful of Reds are tucking into full Englishes.

'Alright lad,' they greet me.

I have to ask who they fancy in round four.

Everton is a popular choice but there are also preferences for Aldershot or Southampton.

Whatever the identity of the Reds' next opponents, Kopites will share the hope that this Carling Cup adventure will only end with another successful trip south in February.

Craig's the Brighton Bell

BRIGHTON & HOVE ALBION 1 LIVERPOOL 2
(Carling Cup 3rd round) Amex Stadium, 21.09.11

GOALS from Craig Bellamy and Dirk Kuyt booked Liverpool's place in the last 16 as the Reds became the first team to win at the Amex Stadium.

A late penalty somehow gave Brighton a fleeting glimpse of a comeback after the Reds had controlled much of the game on their first visit to the Seagulls' new home.

But for the woodwork, Kenny Dalglish's men could have ended the first half four goals to the good.

The attacking quartet of Bellamy, Kuyt, Maxi and Luis Suarez combined cleverly as they interchanged positions during the opening 45 minutes. Their fluid football produced a string of opportunities.

Bellamy broke the deadlock inside seven minutes when a neat passing movement ended with Suarez playing him in on the left of goal. He kept his composure to fire a low angled drive across Casper Ankergren and into the far corner.

From then on, the Brighton keeper's goal led a charmed life.

Just after the half-hour, Bellamy picked out Suarez with a free-kick from the right and his header clipped the far post.

Ten minutes later, Bellamy almost scored a brilliant second when his 35-yard free-kick crashed against the bar with Ankergren rooted to the spot.

And with two minutes of the half remaining, Jay Spearing surged forward and was denied a first Reds goal by the Dane's sprawling save as he pushed it onto the post once again.

Add in another chance that saw Suarez narrowly fail to convert a clever pass from Kuyt and, by the break, Liverpool could have scored the five goals that would have taken them to an all-time tally of 9,000 in all competitions.

That they only scored the once almost proved costly in the opening exchanges of the second period when Brighton tested the strength of the bar themselves. Self-confessed Kopite Craig Noone gave his fellow fans a scare with a fine 20-yard strike.

Those travelling supporters were given a boost when Steven Gerrard made his eagerly awaited return to action for the final quarter of an hour.

And it was Gerrard who started the move which led to Liverpool doubling their advantage nine minutes from time.

His clearance found Bellamy on the left and the Welshman's clever square pass found the onrushing Maxi. He kept the move going by playing in the overlapping Kuyt, who beat Ankergren with a low finish to the delight of the Liverpool fans behind the goal.

Brighton were given hope of a late comeback when they grabbed a 90th minute consolation as Ashley Barnes converted from the penalty spot after Jamie Carragher had brought down ex-Valencia winger Vicente Rodriguez.

But by then Liverpool had done more than enough and were fully deserving of marking their first trip to Brighton's new home with a win.

BRIGHTON (4-2-3-1): Ankergren; Calderon, Greer, Cook, Vincelot; Bridcutt, Navarro (Barnes 77); Buckley (Vicente 60), Noone, Sparrow (K LuaLua 77); Mackail-Smith. Subs not used: Brezovan, Dunk, Taricco, Kasim.

LIVERPOOL (4-4-2): Reina; Kelly (Flanagan 85), Coates, Carragher, Robinson; Kuyt, Spearing, Lucas, Maxi; Suarez (Gerrard 75), Bellamy. Subs not used: Doni, Carroll, Downing, Wilson, Shelvey.

REFEREE: Michael Oliver (Cramlington)
ATTENDANCE: 21,897
BOOKED: Brighton: Navarro (38, foul on Suarez), Sparrow (40, foul on Lucas), Vincelot (66, foul on Kuyt); Liverpool: Spearing (58, foul on Buckley), Lucas (90, foul on LuaLua).

NOW ON TO STOKE CITY

1983

LIVERPOOL 2
MANCHESTER UNITED 1 (AET)

AGAIN Liverpool won the League Cup the hard way, falling behind to a Norman Whiteside goal in the first half.

Alan Kennedy's bouncing effort eluded Gary Bailey and made it 1-1. He later revealed how some of his teammates were laughing when he scored because they thought the shot was so badly struck.

The, by now, familiar period of extra-time eventually led to Liverpool wearing down an injury-hit United.

Whelan curled in a beautiful winner and Paisley was memorably ushered up the steps by his players to collect the cup.

"I was on a cruise with the Norwegian branch of the Liverpool Supporters Club and they presented me with a picture of the goal I scored in that game," Kennedy remembers. "You can see all the Liverpool players laughing – almost in disbelief – that my shot was on target.

"They shouldn't have been: a couple of minutes earlier I'd had a crack from a similar spot that missed by inches, so I was just finding my range. I remember a fantastic game between two closely matched sides."

> 'In a picture I was presented with of my goal you can see all the Liverpool players laughing – almost in disbelief – that my shot was on target'

1. Grobbelaar
2. Neal
6. Hansen
4. Lawrenson
3. A Kennedy
10 Johnston
8. Lee
11. Souness
5. Whelan
9. Rush
7. Dalglish

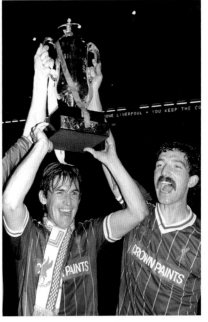

1984

LIVERPOOL 0 EVERTON 0 (AET)
EVERTON 0 LIVERPOOL 1 (R)

A T this point Liverpool's players must have thought the League Cup final was always a game of 120 minutes.

Everton probably edged proceedings in the first all-Merseyside Wembley final, with Alan Hansen's handling of Adrian Heath's shot on the line after just seven minutes going unpunished.

Not even Liverpool's usual Wembley goalscorers of the previous years, Rush and Kennedy could influence the outcome. The former missed the target from almost under the crossbar and the latter had a goal disallowed.

When it all came to an end the familiar opponents were required to meet again nearer to home. Maine Road was the venue for the replay three days later where Graeme Souness' goal secured the cup for the fourth time in a row.

"The replay was dour but memorable for me as I scored," Souness said years later. "I mis-controlled it and had my back to goal but flashed a leg at it and it just dipped in front of Everton

> 'A fan got in the way between me and Bruce Grobbelaar as I passed the trophy down the line but it was all good fun'

keeper Southall before going in.

"It was a bit ad hoc when we were presented with the trophy. A fan got in the way between me and Bruce Grobbelaar as I passed it down the line but it was all good fun."

1. Grobbelaar
2. Neal   6. Hansen
6. Lawrenson
3. A Kennedy
10. Johnston
11. Souness
8. Lee
5. Whelan
9. Rush
7. Dalglish

STOKE EXPECTS...
BUT REDS PREVAIL

SIMON HUGHES took a trip to the Britannia Stadium where the Potters' new breed aren't used to tasting home defeat

SIR STANLEY MA

1915 - 200

AWAYDAYS TO
STOKE CITY FC

TTHEWS CBE

IT'S a prospect few would relish: Stoke City. Away. On a Wednesday night. In November. Okay, it's not quite November but for effect, the 11th month of the year sounds a few degrees colder than the 10th. It's only a few days off anyway. And Stoke City is not a place you want to be in November. Liverpool, indeed, felt the chill last year when they suffered a demoralising 2-0 away day defeat.

Objectively, Stoke is an awkward place to visit any time of the football calendar. Results suggest that. Since becoming a Premier League team in 2008, more than two thirds of their overall points total has come from home matches. In 61 top flight league games at the Britannia Stadium, points have been gained in the form of a draw or a victory in 46 of them. It is not formidable, but for a club that had not appeared in England's top league for 23 years before their latest promotion, it is a highly respectable record. And in nine home games this season before this tie, the Potters remain unbeaten.

So what makes them so difficult? The mantra from their manager, Tony Pulis, is of a traditional, sensible sort: win your home games; do what you can away; then build from there. Tactically, he often deploys central defenders at full-back and in the centre of midfield meaning usually there is only one place up for grabs because of the need to accommodate Rory Delap, he of the throw-in. Glenn Whelan, the best passer at the club occasionally misses out. Further forward, Pulis likes pace and power.

"In many ways, it is such a simple football club," said Matthew Upson, signed in August from West Ham United. "By that, I mean it is straightforward. Everybody knows what they are doing, everybody knows what they are supposed to do, everybody does what they are supposed to do.

"A lot of that stems from the manager. He has the knack of getting the best from everyone. It is a combination of his personality, attitude, decision-making and the ability to recruit the right kind of characters."

Character is important to Pulis. There is no doubt that his squad has plenty of that. There is also a popular belief that another yardstick he judges a player on concerns height. Anyone under six foot need not apply. Pulis accepts there is some truth in this, but denies his team are all about route one. "There is a perception that I always like a big team," he says. "I can remember talking to [former football manager] Alec Stock when I was at Bournemouth. He used to say when his teams walked out he liked to see men, not boys.

"Sometimes managers of teams we have beaten use that as an excuse. The so-called better teams, their managers sometimes had to find a reason why they lost to little old Stoke."

Stoke are evolving. An FA Cup final defeat to Manchester City last May means that this season they are in Europe. And they are performing well, having secured two victories (both at home) and a draw from their three matches so far.

"Stoke are unique," says ex-Liverpool and Stoke forward Howard Gayle. "They play to their strengths in an old fashioned kind of way and they upset people. The more people they upset, the more they enjoy it.

"They play a certain way that may not be to everyone's taste but how anyone can criticise them when they've not just stayed in the Premier League but become an established club that's now competing in Europe, really is beyond me. As long as a team performs within the rules, there is no set way of playing.

"Especially when you consider the teams that have done well in the Europa League over the last few seasons, I really fancy them to do well. They are different to a lot of foreign sides and if they [opponents] don't prepare properly or underestimate them, they'll come unstuck."

Arsenal, it seems, are one of the clubs that Stoke revel in beating. Before a match last season, Arsene Wenger classed it as a clash of ideologies: one side that assumed the ball as a friend, the other one treating it as an afterthought. Visiting supporters chanted about Stoke being a rugby team because of their propensity to maintain possession in the air rather than on the ground. Then Stoke took the lead and extended it, winning 3-1. "Swing Low, Sweet Chariot," came the humorous response from the home end.

It is worth recalling the club's context. Such wit emerges at the gallows. In 1985 - their last spell at the zenith of the English league pyramid before this one - they were relegated with a miserable tally

'Stoke are unique. They play to their strengths in an old fashioned kind of way and they upset people. As long as a team performs within the rules, there is no set way of playing'

- Howard Gayle

Howard Gayle played for the Reds and Stoke

of 17 points. Eleven years ago, Liverpool played a weakened side against them and still won: 8-0. Only in 2005, Pulis, then in his first reign as manager, was sacked by its Icelandic owners for 'failing to exploit foreign markets.'

Off the pitch, The Britannia Stadium, which Stoke moved to in 1997, is one of those locations that invariably, visiting away fans say is "just off the motorway." The type, near the M6 in this case, that you "can't miss." And it's true. It has a modern but generic appearance from the outside. Relocation may have marked progression for the club but its roots will always be at their old Victoria Ground – a home just south of the town centre and a place too that was always difficult to visit. In the 80s, though, the football was different.

"I signed for Stoke because Mick Mills was the manager and he liked his sides to play on the deck," recalls Gayle, who spent three months in the Potteries after a spell playing in America. "Mick was brought up by Bobby Robson at Ipswich and they always played what Mills called 'carpet football.' I was attracted to that because it was what

I was used to at Liverpool. He was an England international and you could see that in the way he professionally went about his business."

Gayle shared a dressing room with Lee Dixon and Steve Bould.

"Both of them later became legends at Arsenal so it tells you a lot about the calibre of player at Stoke. The pitch at Victoria Ground wasn't the best. If you look at any other pitch in the old Second Division, it was probably worse than most of them. But the intention was always there to entertain the crowd and try to pass the ball."

After signing in the March of 1987, Stoke and Gayle missed out on the play-offs by six points.

"We had a good side but Mick couldn't keep the side together because the money wasn't there. It was disappointing because there was a good nucleus. I enjoyed my time [there]. The supporters were excellent and they'd always back the team – just like they do now."

In Gayle's time at the Victoria Ground, the Boothen End was the place where the

POTTERING AROUND:
The sights of Stoke, including the site of the old Victoria Ground and the modern Britannia Stadium

most vocal Stoke supporters stood.

"It was intense," he continues. "Obviously the ground was very different to the new one today – as most old grounds are. In many ways, it was like the Kop at Anfield – a one-tier terrace that generated tremendous noise when full of people."

Today, you could hear a whisper at the original Boothen End. There is a sense that something happened here. But no more. The only clue that Stoke City once resided in this area is the Victoria Pub (still open but for some reason, not this afternoon), with its stand-out red signage.

The old ground has been flattened. Where once performed Sir Stanley Matthews and Gordon Banks now rests abandoned fire hydrants and a field of weeds, some left for so long that they have grown to be the length of at least two Peter Crouches. The scene is curiously depressing. But football moves on. Stoke certainly have.

While the Victoria Ground nestled in a mainly residential area between terraced houses and small businesses like car

>>

washes and scooter repair shops, the new stadium, less than a mile-and-a-half away, is next to a major supermarket distribution centre and an incineration plant. Plumes of smoke are pumped into the already dank evening sky.

The Britannia retains some links with history. Surrounding streets are named after the aforementioned club legends in Matthews and Banks, as well as George Eastham. There's also an impressive Matthews statue. The home end of the ground has been christened the Boothen End under which is housed the Delilah Bar after the fans' favourite anthem. By contrast, the away crowd are placed in the less romantically named Marston's Pedigree Stand.

There is an expectancy here: Stoke might beat Liverpool for the third time in as many home matches. You can see the desire in the eyes of the supporters; in the way they talk over their pre-game pints. They are comfortable in the Premier League now; with a manager and just as importantly, a chairman in Peter Coates they believe in, who like Jack Walker once of Blackburn, is pumping generous amounts of money into his local club. Pulis calls Coates, "a dream."

"He is not only a smashing person, a loyal person, but he knows his football as well and he is sensible with it."

On transfer deadline day, Coates sanctioned the purchase of ex-Liverpool striker Peter Crouch – the reported £12m fee being a club record signing.

"I've had the hard sell from Woody [Jonathan Woodgate] all summer, telling me how much I'd like it here," said Crouch. "Tony Pulis worked extremely hard to get me here and hopefully I will be able to repay him."

"The future seems bright for Stoke."

As it transpired later that evening, that future will have to wait.

MATCH DAY TEAMSHEET
12 SEASON

Stoke City vs Liverpool
Wednesday 26th October 2011 | Kick Off 7.45pm
Carling Cup Round 4
Match Sponsors: Elitis Consultancy

STOKE CITY	LIVERPOOL
Thomas SORENSEN 29	25 Pepe REINA
Robert HUTH 4	34 Martin KELLY
(C) Ryan SHAWCROSS 17	23 Jamie CARRAGHER (C)
Jonathan WOODGATE 39	16 Sebastien COATES
Marc WILSON 12	5 Daniel AGGER
Ryan SHOTTON 30	14 Jordan HENDERSON
Rory DELAP 24	21 LUCAS
Glenn WHELAN 6	20 Jay SPEARING
Matthew ETHERINGTON 26	11 Maxi RODRIGUEZ
Kenwyne JONES 9	7 Luis SUAREZ
Jonathan WALTERS 19	9 Andy CARROLL

Substitutes	Substitutes
Carlo NASH 27	32 DONI
Salif DIAO 15	6 Fabio AURELIO
Jermaine PENNANT 16	18 Dirk KUYT
Matthew UPSON 20	26 Charlie ADAM
Peter CROUCH 25	37 Martin SKRTEL
Cameron JEROME 33	38 Jonathan FLANAGAN
Wilson PALACIOS 40	39 Craig BELLAMY

MATCH OFFICIALS
Referee I. Probert | Assistants D Bryan & C Richards | Fourth Official J Moss

THE MATCH

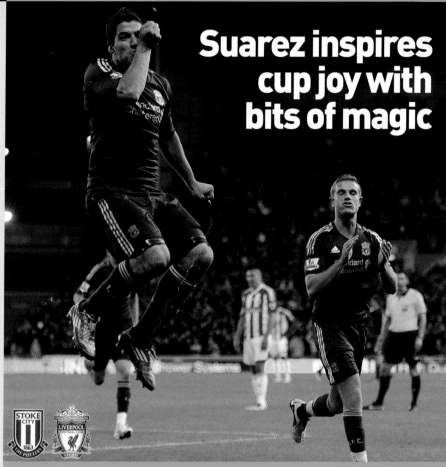

Suarez inspires cup joy with bits of magic

STOKE CITY 1 LIVERPOOL 2 (Carling Cup 4th round) Britannia Stadium, 26.10.11

STOKE are never more frustrating to play than when they are 1-0 up. The crowd, spurred on by the sight of a goal become frenzied; they squall at every tackle; they cheer every set-piece with even more vigour than usual. The players out there harry. They become an even more difficult opponent than they were already.

But not for Luis Suarez. For him, the subduing of a team, the silencing of a stadium, is a mission. He lives for situations like this. Here, he succeeded. He didn't win this match for Liverpool on his own, but his response to Stoke's opener was exceptional. As Tony Pulis jotted in his programme notes: people have been 'going on about' Suarez – and 'with good reason.'

Before the Uruguayan's intervention, Liverpool couldn't score. Six times in the first half they may have taken the lead. But where Suarez and others missed from six yards, he scored from 20, almost as if a tap-in is beneath the man.

"I ran out of words to describe him after a week when he came to our club," said Kenny Dalglish. "He could have taken one before that and maybe it would have been more comfortable for us, but it was worth waiting for."

Suarez struck first just when Liverpool needed inspiring most. Shortly after the break he sprung his special move: the nutmeg - this one on Ryan Shotton - before curling with such grace beyond Thomas Sorensen that even some Stoke supporters clapped.

Later, with extra-time looming even more ominously than usual on a chilly Staffordshire night, he finished the hosts off with another expertly taken goal, this time with his head. Somehow, the striker was left all alone in the box. Maybe his movement was just too good. In celebration, Suarez kissed the Liverpool badge, fell to the ground and most of his team-mates piled on top.

It wasn't just about Suarez, of course. There were other protagonists behind this victory. Daniel Agger, imperious at left-back; Jay Spearing and Lucas dominated midfield and Andy Carroll, linked intelligently with runners from deep. The general performance of the Liverpool team was encouraging. Few teams recover from a goal down at Stoke and win.

The visitors started briskly. Carroll connected with a corner. The Geordie then fired straight at Sorensen from distance before Suarez could only connect awkwardly with the rebound.

At the other end, the tactical plan was hardly inconspicuous. Stoke responded, as they do, from a set-piece and the resulting scrimmage. The turquoise markings revealed that the pitch had been shortened and narrowed. Winning throw-ins and corners were, indeed, Stoke's priority. From a Rory Delap hurl – the ball fell to Shotton; the deputy throw-in specialist in the team. The centre-back, converted to the right hand side of midfield for this match, could only screw wide.

With Spearing in the centre, Liverpool's retention of possession was quick. He fed Suarez and checking inside, the Uruguayan tried to fool Sorensen. But the goalkeeper read the lob.

Suarez's best chance came when he connected with Lucas' square pass. Sorensen, again, was ready to smother – just as he did moments later from Carroll.

Liverpool were entirely dominant. But it was Stoke who took the lead. Shortly before the half-time whistle, Jonathan Walters crossed for Kenwyne Jones and at full stretch, he headed past Pepe Reina.

There was still time for another Liverpool opportunity. Suarez could have tumbled in the box under a challenge from Ryan Shawcross but he stayed on his feet and the chance was gone.

Craig Bellamy, on as a substitute, hit a post in the second half but Suarez's contribution was most telling. It was also unsurprising. "The first goal was just fantastic and a bit of brilliance from Luis," said Jordan Henderson. "But we are used to that because we see it all the time."

STOKE (4-4-2): Sorensen; Huth, Wilson, Woodgate, Shawcross; Shotton (Pennant, 60), Delap, Whelan, Etherington (Jerome, 63); Jones (Crouch, 87), Walters. Subs not used: Nash, Diao, Upson, Palacios

LIVERPOOL (4-4-2): Reina; Kelly, Carragher (Skrtel, 46), Coates, Agger; Henderson, Lucas, Spearing, Maxi (Bellamy, 81); Suarez (Kuyt, 87), Carroll. Subs not used: Doni, Aurelio, Adam, Flanagan

REFEREE: Lee Probert
ATTENDANCE: 24, 934
BOOKED: **Liverpool:** Carragher (foul 21) **Stoke:** Shawcross (foul 41), Whelan (unsporting conduct 55), Huth (dissent 89)

LEAGUE CUP WINNERS 1995 & 2001

1995

**LIVERPOOL 2
BOLTON WANDERERS 1**

STEVE McManaman bewitched Bolton with a couple of stunning solo goals as the Reds claimed a record fifth League Cup triumph.

His first arrived eight minutes before the break when he ran on to John Barnes' pass, drifted outside Alan Stubbs and inside Scott Green before side-footing past goalkeeper Keith Branagan.

Midway through the second half another successful solo slalom saw him ghost past Green, Jason McAteer and Mark Seagraves before curling a low right-foot shot beyond Branagan.

Alan Thompson hooked in a reply for the Football League side but it was Liverpool captain Ian Rush who lifted the trophy.

"We were well in control and as usual we put ourselves under pressure by conceding a goal," recalls midfielder Jamie Redknapp. "The buzz at the final whistle was immense. It was my first trophy for Liverpool and in the end, we deserved to win."

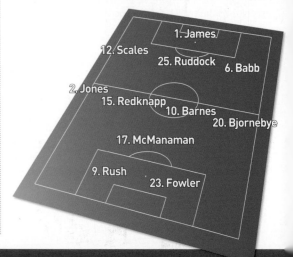

1. James
12. Scales
25. Ruddock
6. Babb
2. Jones
15. Redknapp
10. Barnes
20. Bjornebye
17. McManaman
9. Rush
23. Fowler

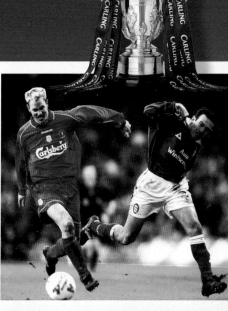

2001

LIVERPOOL 1-1 BIRMINGHAM CITY
(LIVERPOOL WON 5-4 ON PENS)

D ARREN Purse equalised for Birmingham after Robbie Fowler's early opener. Andy Johnson later missed the decisive penalty.

Jamie Carragher had scored his seconds before. "It was sudden death but I didn't have any nerves," Carragher said. "I knew where I wanted to put it and thankfully it went in. My dad missed the moment, though. He left his seat because he couldn't watch.

'Gerard Houllier told us to remember how winning felt and urged us to use it as an inspiration. It was and we did'

"It had been a difficult game but we battled through and deserved it. It was my first trophy with the senior Liverpool team and it was the catalyst for us to go on and win the cup treble.

"Gerard Houllier told us to remember how winning felt and urged us to use it as an inspiration. It was and we did."

1. Westerveld
6 Babbel   2. Henchoz
            12. Hyypia
                23. Carragher
25. Biscan   17. Gerrard
              16. Hamann
                7. Smicer
9. Fowler
        8. Heskey

BRIDGE OF HIGHS AS REDS DO DOUBLE

Continuing our series of 2011/12 Carling Cup road trips, JOHN HYNES followed Reds fans to the home of Chelsea – a venue that is fast becoming a favourite for the travelling Kop·

AWAYDAYS TO
CHELSEA FC

Lime Street
Station and Subway

Euston Station

VALID ONLY WITH TRAVEL TICKET

Class	Ticket Type		
STD SEAT		Start Date	Price
		29·NOV·11	£0·00W
From			
LIVERPOOL L ST *		Number	
		41212	0452AP7530
To			
LONDON EUSTON *		Valid at	
Coach	Seat	1048 HOURS ON 29·NOV·11	
C	34		

SEAT RESERVATION
KD319418

RTN
0452AP7530

From			
LONDON TERMINALS	Valid Until 28·DMR·11	Validity AS ADVERTISED	
To	Route ANY PERMITTED	Price £70·00W	
LIVERPOOL STNS *	2-PART RETURN		

MR JOHN HYNES

KD319418

WE'VE got a game in Lndn last wk of Nov. Am I ok to stay at yours?' That was the gist of many text messages at the end of October 2011.

After triumphing against Stoke thanks to some Luis Suarez magic we were all looking to the draw for the last eight of the Carling Cup. Inevitably we were paired alongside Chelsea, a fixture that left most of us not knowing whether to laugh or grimace in frustration.

'No worries. Who ye playing?' was the reply to my original request.

When I told my mate with no interest in footy the response was: 'Chelsea again?' Somebody who doesn't know or care about the sport responding in that way is more confirmation – as if it's required - that we've played the Londoners far, far too often.

Another trip to Stamford Bridge wasn't something you could approach with relish, especially after facing them in a league game there just nine days earlier.

That was part of the reason why I wasn't over-confident about our chances of progress. When was the last time we twice defeated a rival away from home in such a short space of time? Not too many answers or recollections of similar historical precedents were forthcoming.

Yet, with a place in the semi-final the prize for the winners, the train tickets for the capital were booked.

Lime Street on a Tuesday morning is buzzing with activity, although there is little trace of any Kopites awaiting the 10.48 train to Euston. There is the odd red and white scarf in view but that's it. Perhaps the fans have heeded Kenny Dalglish's warning of thinking carefully before travelling as he isn't sure what kind of side will be used just 48 hours after a keenly contested draw with Man City.

On the train there is little football-related chat, with the old couple sitting across

from me journeying south for Christmas shopping rather than to watch the match. 'How do you improve your memory?' the woman asks in relation to a newspaper article she is reading in the Daily Mail. 'By not talking too much,' is her husband's quick-witted answer.

The same paper carries a feature focusing on our seven previous League Cup successes, five at Wembley and two in Cardiff.

Phil Thompson explains how the trophy was left on the bus after our first victory in 1981, a replay win over West Ham at Villa Park courtesy of goals by Dalglish and Alan Hansen.

Before walking out at the revamped Wembley for the first time could be even contemplated though we had to progress past Andre Villas-Boas' men.

The omens going in to the tie were

> ## 'There is the odd red and white scarf in view but that's it'

mixed. On the last three occasions we've reached a final, the 2005 and 2007 Champions League, with the FA Cup showpiece in between those continental journeys, we've defeated Chelsea along the way.

The flip side is our last quarter-final appearance in anything came against the same opposition in the 2009 Champions League and we exited on a 7-5 aggregate scoreline.

Our most recent last eight appearance in this competition also saw a defeat at Stamford Bridge, with Peter Crouch dismissed. A glance at the line-up from that night shows Charles Itandje and

Andriy Voronin played. It was also the only time we've failed to score in our last 41 outings in this competition. Having read all those stats I ask myself why we bother searching for omens before a game.

More taxing than finding that info is recalling when we last faced the Londoners when it wasn't live on TV. It's certainly a long time ago.

Maybe the TV companies have grown as bored by this fixture as us, or maybe they are taking on the attitude that 'it's only the League Cup'.

With no European fixtures on our calendar for 2011/12 Kenny certainly hasn't adopted that approach. In each round the Scot has picked a strong side. Suarez started at St James' Park, the AMEX and the Britannia. Pepe Reina has also featured in all those ties.

And when you consider he had only made a solitary appearance in this competition in the previous half-a-dozen years it's an example of the importance we're placing on the first available silverware of the season.

Of course Kenny is no stranger to success in the tournament, playing a part in our four consecutive victories between 1981 and 1984. He hasn't won it as a manager, so adding it to the leagues and FA Cups he's won is also a motivation.

Doing well in it can clearly shape a season. Our third and fourth European Cups had been preceded by success in the Milk Cup weeks earlier.

In 2001 it was the first of three cups in a season, and, although we lost the 2005 final against tonight's opponents, going so close to winning it in Cardiff surely gave the players added belief as they went on to knock out Chelsea before collecting the European Cup in Turkey.

Predicting the team for tonight's tie isn't easy. It's not as difficult as finding somewhere to have a drink near Stamford Bridge though. The tube journey from Euston to Fulham Broadway, taking the Victoria line and then the District line, was simple but most pubs in the area are only admitting home supporters.

It means the away contingent huddle together near the Bovril Gate entrance to the stadium. Carra will surely be back in the side they all agree, perhaps alongside Seb Coats [Coates], as some call him. Jay Spearing is a certainty to play and Craig Bellamy too.

Villas-Boas, or AVB as certain sections of the press have christened the Portuguese, has used some of the youngsters at his disposal in these

MAKING THE HEADLINES: The Daily Mail on the day of the game, Luis Garcia celebrates semi-final success against Chelsea, Peter Crouch was sent off in 2007 and Luis Suarez was the hero against Stoke in the previous round

games so far. Though, after losing two of his previous three fixtures, it would be no surprise to see him move away from that policy.

Ray Wilkins was once a 'young man' at the Blues and is spotted as he steps out of a taxi, manages to 'stay on his feet' and walks into the ground.

Another ex-member of the Chelsea backroom staff will also certainly be here tonight. 'Welcome home Clarkey' is the shout as first-team coach Steve Clarke steps off the LFC bus. He's followed by the likes of Suarez, Reina, Kuyt, Carra, Adam, Lucas, Enrique, Johnson, Carroll, Downing, Henderson and Kelly. Clearly Kenny has brought his strongest squad.

Inside the almost-empty ground the few home supporters present rush to the front of the stand when they spot the cup-tied Raul Meireles walking down the touchline. His very early arrival for a game he isn't eligible to play in conveniently means he doesn't have to pass the soon-to-be full away end.

While the goalkeepers go through warm-up routines the press room is full with journalists and pundits doing their own pre-match preparations, which mainly consist of eating some of the fine roast dinner on offer.

That's followed by a selection of cheeses and crackers and various cakes. Confirming the fact that most people who report on football have the mindset of kids there is also a choice of sweets, with M&Ms proving the most popular.

The appearance of the team-sheets sees the eating end and some furious typing begin. Via Twitter, Facebook and various other websites the line-ups quickly reach the public. The immediate impression is Liverpool have named a stronger side.

Bellamy and Carroll up front, with Carra back in for the first time since the last round and Maxi returning. Ross Turnbull, Ryan Bertrand, Josh McEachran and Romelu Lukaku all start for the hosts. AVB (even I'm writing it now) has been true to his word.

When the players emerge for the [not on TV] 7.45 kick-off David Luiz is pointing towards the heavens. Charlie Adam is wearing a hat to protect him from the cold as he takes his place in the dugout.

A minute of applause for the recently deceased Gary Speed rings around the ground. Bellamy is understandably affected by the moment as he wipes tears from his face. Enrique comes to the bench to change his boots as the teams get ready.

Phil Dowd receives some stick from the home fans and we haven't even started yet. Maybe they've heard that we haven't lost on any of the last half-a-dozen times he's taken charge of our games. Another [pointless] omen.

'On the train there is little football chat. An old couple travel to shop rather than go the match'

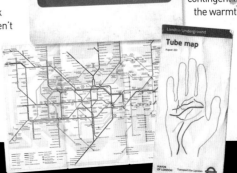

Two minutes in and the Stoke-born official is being booed even louder. Luiz goes down after Coates slides in and no penalty is given. It's the first incident of what will be an eventful night for the unmissable Chelsea defender.

He continues to tangle with opponents on and off the ball and looks certain to pick up a red card if he carries on in such a manner.

Not even a penalty miss by Carroll can quieten the away supporters who are easily out-singing the other three sides of the ground. Kenny is struggling to make himself heard as he attempts to chat to Kelly on the touchline while McEachran gets treatment.

The Liverpool fans chant Carroll's name before gleefully welcoming the ball in amongst them after a Lampard shot finishes high up in the Shed End.

Fernando Torres' endeavours inevitably attract attention, especially when he is challenged by one of his former team-mates. Kelly, Carra and Lucas all hit him with well-timed and strong tackles.

Suddenly Luiz's surges forward have halted. Maybe with half-time approaching his manager wants to ensure it's reached without the hosts conceding.

The interval sees the media contingent make their way to the warmth of the press room. It also provides a chance to top up on M&Ms as the penalty appeals dominate the conversation.

Resumption of the

>>

The Shed End

action sees no substitutions and Torres wildly attempt to tackle Bellamy. The Welshman looks threatening as he drifts around the field, never staying in one place for too long.

One run leads to him just over-hitting a pass to play Carroll in. Another good attack halts when he shoots over. Chelsea can't seem to keep a track of his movement.

That area of Torres' game seems less threatening until he earns a free-kick on the right. Lampard floats it across to Florent Malouda who awkwardly volleys the ball in to the turf, where it spins up and lands on the crossbar before dropping in the six yard box. Luiz looks set to bundle it in until Coates makes a decent block with his chest. 'Handball' those behind the goal moan. The Chelsea bench scream at fourth official Lee Mason.

Suddenly more space seems to be available at either end as Maxi leads a counter-attack, which is only stopped by a good tackle in the box. Villas-Boas is on his haunches as he views the unfolding action.

Bellamy is now out on the right flank as he again escapes the attentions of the

home side. His position has been spotted by Henderson though, and his pass locates the number 39 in space. Quickly he breaks forward as Maxi simultaneously bursts in to the box. The square ball across takes Turnbull out of the equation and the Argentine has scored against Chelsea away again.

His joy is understandable. The goalscorer, along with fellow South Americans Lucas and Coates, even indulges in a humorous dance before pointing to the name on the back of his shirt.

Chelsea are still regrouping when Bellamy is on the left flank, winning a free-kick in a dangerous position. He takes it and bends a superb delivery into the box where Kelly – yet to open his scoring account as the programme reminded us - heads the ball in. His enthusiastic celebrations illustrate what it means to him as his England U21 team-mate Henderson sprints over to join the celebrations.

A spell of LFC possession is enjoyed with a wall of noise cascading down from the away supporters. Bellamy continues to threaten as he hits a long-range free-

kick on target before Lucas goes down injured.

Play continues until Maxi boots the ball out and in to the press box. Radio Merseyside's Mike Hughes attempts to return it, but his throw fails to reach the playing surface. Instead a fan chucks the ball back, with it landing on the medical bag of LFC first-team doctor Zaf Iqbal.

Worryingly it becomes obvious that Lucas won't be returning to action as he departs on a stretcher to be replaced by Adam.

Villas-Boas whistles and shouts at his players as he tries to stir a comeback. Substitute Anelka looks like he might score until Reina expertly rushes from the line and thwarts his advance. The defence complete the job by clearing the Frenchman's cross.

Dalglish withdraws Bellamy and gives him a hug. His departure is greeted in a different fashion by the Chelsea fans. They are still clinging to some hope when Alex lines up a free-kick in a similar place to where he scored from against us in the Champions League in '09. When it flies wide it's the cue for those in blue to exit en masse. The Suarez song rings in their ears as they do so.

Maxi is another recipient of a hug from the boss as he makes way to let Skrtel on. The Slovak's introduction coincides with the fourth official's board telling us four minutes remain. Jose Bosingwa's cross harmlessly drifting out for a goal-kick confirms it's going to be a comfortable injury-time for us. Villas-Boas stares into the distance. He's stopped dishing out instructions.

Then Torres gains possession in a dangerous position. Reina advances as the offside flag goes up. The striker still opts to shoot, blazing the ball over the bar. It's the conclusion to our third win at this ground in 2011.

As the whistle sounds, substitute goalkeeper Doni stops for a chat with Chelsea's Brazilians, Alex and Ramires. Nearby Dalglish, Clarke and Kevin Keen share high fives and embraces with the players on the pitch. Reina sprays unused sub Suarez with Lucozade.

The familiar 'de ne ne ne ne ne ne ne ne ne ne ne' tune of the Batman TV show emerges from near the pressbox. It's a home supporter, who has swapped the superhero's name for that of Spackman. Nigel, the ex-Chelsea and Liverpool player, is commentating for Radio City and grins as he's serenaded.

It all means I might be looking for another place to stay in London at the end of February.

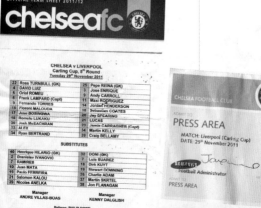

THE MATCH

Bridge holds no fear for Reds

CHELSEA 0 LIVERPOOL 2 (Carling Cup quarter-final) Stamford Bridge, 29.11.11

A TRIP to Wembley moved closer as Kenny Dalglish's side stretched the Scot's unbeaten run against Chelsea to 13 games.

Maxi Rodriguez's second goal at Stamford Bridge in less than a fortnight and a Martin Kelly header sent Liverpool through to the Carling Cup semi-final against Man City.

Andy Carroll also had a penalty saved by Ross Turnbull as spot-kick appeals were the talking point of the opening period.

The first shouts for an award were heard with only two minutes elapsed. David Luiz's forward burst ended when he went to ground under a Sebastian Coates challenge. With the home fans screaming 'foul', Phil Dowd booked the Brazilian for diving. The defender didn't protest, even shaking the official's hand in acceptance of the decision.

Shortly after, Luiz was at the heart of another shout for a spot-kick, this time at the other end as he appeared to nudge Carroll.

Soon enough there was a penalty. Carroll claimed his header had struck the hand of Alex. Dowd initially didn't listen, then eventually took the loud protests on board, indicated there had been an infringement and booked the Chelsea man.

Carroll grabbed the ball, and after a discussion with Craig Bellamy, struck a

shot that Turnbull pushed away. Another spot-kick could also have been awarded when Luiz clearly tripped the Liverpool number nine later in the half. This time Dowd waved play on.

The frantic nature of the contest continued into the second half, without either keeper having much to do. Both teams got in threatening positions only for the final pass to let them down each time.

Chelsea almost scored when a Frank Lampard free-kick led to Florent Malouda's bouncing effort coming back off the bar and Coates scrambling Luiz's follow-up away.

The home supporters upped the volume in anticipation of a breakthrough materialising. It did, but not as they hoped. Henderson found Bellamy on the right and his pass for Maxi across the six-yard box was perfect to tap in.

Immediately Nicolas Anelka and Juan Mata were prepared to come on. As they stood waiting to enter the action Bellamy floated in a free-kick. It found the unmarked Kelly, who nodded in.

A quick reply was needed if the hosts were to have any hope. It never looked likely. Anelka escaped behind the defence only for Pepe Reina to dash off his line and delay the striker. The Spaniard also caught a Fernando Torres header.

Liverpool repelled most attacks comfortably, with Coates and Jamie Carragher consistently getting in the way. Long before the end the Stamford Bridge faithful were exiting.

CHELSEA (4-1-2-3): Cech, Bosingwa, Luiz, Alex, Bertrand, Lampard, Romeu, McEachran (Ramires 42), Malouda (Anelka 64), Lukaku (Mata 64), Torres. Unused subs: Hilario, Ivanovic, Ferreira, Kalou.

LIVERPOOL (4-2-3-1): Reina, Kelly, Coates, Carragher, Enrique, Henderson, Spearing, Lucas (Adam 70), Maxi (Skrtel 89), Bellamy (Kuyt 79), Carroll. Unused subs: Doni, Suarez, Downing, Flanagan

REFEREE: P. Dowd

ATTENDANCE: 40, 511

BOOKED: Chelsea: Luiz (3, diving), Alex (21, handball), Malouda (34, foul), Bertrand (44, foul), Ramires (66, foul) Liverpool: Coates (54, foul)

2003

LIVERPOOL 2
MANCHESTER UNITED 0

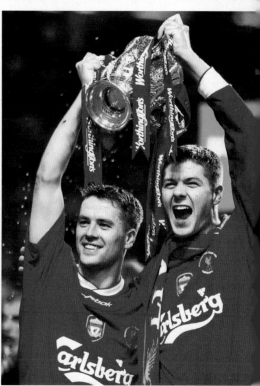

THIS was the most comfortable of final wins thanks to goals from Steven Gerrard and Michael Owen.

Goalkeeper Jerzy Dudek was nominated man of the match only a few months after his errors were largely to blame for a league loss to United at Anfield.

"I told Jerzy three days ago 'I can feel you will be the hero.'" Gerard Houllier said. "Today he was man of the match. But football can be like that. Sometimes you can be at the bottom and then be a hero again. I just had a feeling.

"I'm a great believer that when you have the right attitude everything else follows. He had a good run after the World Cup but then he made some mistakes and we had to support him."

'I told Jerzy three days ago 'I can feel you will be the hero.' Today he was man of the match. But football can be like that. Sometimes you can be at the bottom and then be a hero again. I just had a feeling'

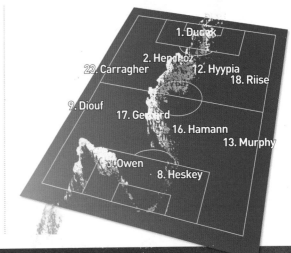

1. Dudek

2. Henchoz

23. Carragher   12. Hyypia

18. Riise

9. Diouf

17. Gerrard

16. Hamann

13. Murphy

Owen

8. Heskey

THE REDS' WELL TRODDEN PATH

The journey to Manchester might not be packed with mystique but CHRIS McLOUGHLIN saw Kenny's men travel to The Etihad to tee up a trip to Wembley

THE Manchester Ship Canal. The Liverpool to Manchester Railway. The East Lancashire Road. The M62. Even without being able to book a direct flight between John Lennon International Airport and Manchester Ringway, there are plenty of different ways to travel between the North-West's two biggest cities. And it's just as well.

Between January 3 and February 11, Liverpool played Manchester City and Manchester United five times. The two Premier League trips to Manchester could've gone better, but we didn't half have a good day when United came to Anfield in the FA Cup.

The other two games – when the Carling Cup gains an extra leg for the semi-final – were the biggest matches ever played between Liverpool and Manchester City. Think about it.

We'd met 163 times before, but never in a cup final and only once in a semi-final, the 1981 League Cup. Aside from the 1971/72 and 1976/77 campaigns, when the Reds and Sky Blues were competing for the league title (Derby County won it in '72, Liverpool in '77), we've never really been major rivals, largely because City were rarely in the hunt for silverware during our glory days.

Things are different now. City ended their 35-year wait for a trophy with the FA Cup last season and with untold riches allowing Roberto Mancini to build their strongest ever squad, the Premier League title may be on its way to The Etihad.

But City aren't the only upwardly mobile club. Under the ownership of Fenway Sports Group and management of Kenny Dalglish, it feels like a successful new era at Anfield is imminent.

Kenny has restored the feelgood factor. Talented, young, hungry players have been attracted to Anfield. There's a buzz of anticipation about Kopites. But there's something missing. Silverware.

It has been said that only when Steven Gerrard gets his hands on a trophy again will the next stage of Liverpool Football

Club's redevelopment be complete.

And here we are. As you well know, 'win a trophy' is a box that was ticked off against Cardiff City at Wembley, but cast your mind back to January, before we played City over two legs.

Mancini's men were top of the Premier League. The had a 100% home record in the PL – winning every game by at least two clear goals – and could boast of 6-1 and 5-1 away wins at Old Trafford and White Hart Lane. Liverpool couldn't possibly have faced a harder semi-final.

At least it was an easy trip for the 6,000-plus travelling Kopites. Having made a day (and night) of it in Exeter, Brighton and London, Manchester was a 'get in and out' job for most Reds.

I spent the day in the office and drove to Manchester. Don't all get excited at once.

I'd love to tell you tales of Scousers sailing gondolas down the Ship Canal,

'A cheeky chant of 'you couldn't sell all yer tickets' rang out'

Mancunian bars rocking with Reds and Liver Bird banners being draped off the Rovers Return, but let's be realistic.

The first leg of a League Cup semi-final in Manchester isn't the same as going to the FA Cup semi-final at a neutral venue or travelling away in Europe.

It was, however, the gateway to Wembley and a night when Liverpool's travelling contingent showed their hosts what support is all about.

Less that 30,000 City fans turned up at The Etihad. Maybe the dismal Manchester weather, the game being screened lived on BBC1 or economic factors put them off?

Whatever the reason, the stage-managed pre-match show of the floodlights being switched off and a giant blue moon rising on the big screen was overshadowed by a rousing rendition of You'll Never Walk Alone.

A cheeky chant of 'you couldn't sell all yer tickets, sell all yer tickets' followed shortly after. The travelling Kop had the upper hand, and so did Kenny Dalglish.

Kenny did an Italian job on Mancini. He turn the Carling Cup semi-final into a tight European encounter, but only after Liverpool took the lead.

The mere mention of Joe Hart now has Kopites everywhere grasping their heads and groaning with an anguished look. City's outstanding keeper appears to be on a personal mission to make more saves from Liverpool players than any other goalie in the history of football. He'd turn the kitchen sink over his bar if you threw it at him.

It took a Stevie G penalty to beat him at The Etihad with the sight of the ball hitting the net prompting wild celebrations in the away end. "We're on the march with Kenny's army..."

Five minutes later a hamstring injury to Jay Spearing forced him off and it disrupted the Reds. City began to get a foothold, missing a couple of decent chances, and the old nerves started to jangle a bit.

In the second half, Kenny pulled his Italian job, with Jose Enrique and Jamie Carragher brought on to counter Mancini's attacking substitutions.

Some Kopites in the Etihad away end were a tad frustrated at Liverpool's caution in the second half, but most realised it was a shrewd move by the manager.

City created less than a potter with a wonky wheel in an earthquake and the Reds became the first side to stop them scoring in a home game since November 2010, having lost 3-0 there eight days earlier. It put into perspective what a good victory it was for Liverpool.

As I walked back to the car with the wind whistling around the now empty outdoor bars in the Etihad Campus, the road to Wembley crossed my mind.

Exeter. Brighton. Stoke. London. Manchester. We were 90 minutes from a long-awaited return to Wembley, but only if we could avoid defeat in a city we'd yet to play in.

And when that city is Liverpool, where the Reds had only ever lost one Anfield semi-final, to Leeds in the 1971 European Fairs Cup, I couldn't help but think all roads lead to Wembley.

And they did.

Carling Cup Semi-Final
Wed 11 January 2012 19:45

Manchester City FC vs Liverpool FC

Visiting Supporter   05898318
Aisle: Block:118 Row: G   Seat: 498
Entrance: M   Price: 35.00

ETIHAD

ADULT

05898318
Valid for adult unless stub removed

The main man for semi-finals

MANCHESTER CITY 0 LIVERPOOL 1, Carling Cup semi-final 1st leg, Etihad Stadium 11.01.12

LIVERPOOL put themselves on course to return to Wembley for the first time since 1996 thanks to this fine 1-0 Carling Cup semi-final first-leg victory at Manchester City.

A sound defensive display was the basis for the win, although it took some good goalkeeping from both Joe Hart and Pepe Reina to ensure Steven Gerrard's penalty was the only goal of the game.

Gerrard has now scored the winning goal in three consecutive League Cup semi-finals – the previous two coming against Watford in 2005.

For Liverpool to be within 90 minutes of the final having yet to play at Anfield was quite remarkable. Victory at The Etihad meant that Kenny Dalglish's side had won five consecutive away games in the League Cup this season – a club record – and they fully deserved to return from Manchester with a first leg lead.

As much as anything, it was a tactical victory for Dalglish. Having seen his side lose 3-0 at City in the Premier League eight days earlier, he changed things around.

Martin Kelly came in at right-back, Glen Johnson switched to the left to counter Adam Johnson's penchant for cutting inside from the right wing and Gerrard and Craig Bellamy both started to add power and pace in midfield.

It allowed Liverpool to control the game from the start and they could have been two or three up in the opening 15 minutes, but for some fine keeping from Hart.

The City goalkeeper denied Andy Carroll in the fifth minute after he'd shrugged off Stefan Savic to latch onto Stewart Downing's through-ball and dived to his left five minutes later to push Gerrard's drive past the post.

From the resulting corner he produced an even better save when Daniel Agger flicked Downing's volley goalwards with his heel.

Liverpool's pressure finally paid off when Savic raked his studs down Agger's right knee from Gerrard's corner. Lee Mason pointed to the spot, Gerrard stepped up and slotted the ball into the net, low to Joe Hart's right.

Pepe Reina made an important save in the 43rd minute when he dived left to push away Samir Nasri's shot and James Milner missed a sitter, but City struggled to break Liverpool down.

Kenny made a number of tactical alterations in the second half after Sergio Aguero had ran on to Kelly's backpass in the 56th minute only for Reina to narrow the angle.

Well aware that City had scored in every home game this season, including twice the weekend before against Manchester United

despite being 3-0 down and only having 10 men, the Liverpool boss later admitted he wanted to "batten down the hatches."

Jose Enrique's arrival signalled a shift to a 5-4-1 formation with Glen Johnson playing in an unorthodox floating left-sided centre-half role and Jamie Carragher coming on in midfield.

Reina made a good save when Micah Richards headed a Nasri corner goalwards, but the Reds saw out the game easily.

MANCHESTER CITY (4-2-3-1): Hart, Richards, Clichy, Lescott, Savic, De Jong (Kolarov 72), Barry, Milner, A Johnson (Dzeko 66), Balotelli (Nasri 39), Aguero. Subs not used: Pantilimon, Zabaleta, Hargreaves, Onuoha.

LIVERPOOL (4-2-3-1): Reina, Kelly, G Johnson, Agger, Skrtel, Spearing (Adam 23), Gerrard, Downing (Jose Enrique 59), Bellamy (Carragher 79), Henderson, Carroll.
Subs not used: Doni, Coates, Kuyt, Shelvey.

REFEREE: Lee Mason (Bolton)
ATTENDANCE: 36,017
BOOKED: Liverpool: Carragher (86, foul), Manchester City: Nasri (86, retaliation),

>>

We're all going to Wem-ber-ley

LIVERPOOL 2 MANCHESTER CITY 2, Carling Cup semi-final 2nd leg, Anfield, 25.01.12

KENNY'S army were on the march to Wembley for the first time since 1996 after seeing off Manchester at Anfield.

With a crucial 1-0 first leg victory secured at The Etihad a fortnight earlier thanks to a Steven Gerrard penalty, the Reds knew that a draw would be good enough to take them to their first Carling Cup final since 2005.

But anyone expecting Liverpool to shut up shop to try and protect their one-goal advantage was hugely mistaken. Roared on by a noisy, passionate Anfield crowd, Kenny Dalglish's side attacked City at every opportunity and only an inspired display of goalkeeping from Joe Hart prevented the Reds from comfortably winning the game.

Dirk Kuyt and Stewart Downing came back into the side for Maxi Rodriguez and Andy Carroll and it was the former Aston Villa winger who created Liverpool's first goalscoring opportunity in the fourth minute.

Aleksandar Kolarov only managed to clear Downing's cross straight to Jose Enrique in the penalty area, but the Liverpool left-back was denied his first goal in a red shirt when Hart blocked his shot with his toe. Downing blasted the rebound wide.

With the noise levels inside Anfield reminiscent of a big European night, Liverpool, with Gerrard giving a disciplined display in the holding midfield role, pressed City - who started with an unusual 3-2-4-1 formation - and continued to create chances.

Charlie Adam's shot from the edge of the box was saved by Hart, the energetic Craig Bellamy volleyed over from Kuyt's chest-down and, after cleverly turning the nervy Stefan Savic on the edge of the box, Bellamy saw Hart push away another effort.

At the other end, Edin Dzeko felt he should have had a penalty after being challenged by Adam, but Pepe Reina was relatively untroubled until the 31st minute when the visitors opened the scoring against the run of play.

Nigel De Jong had only ever scored once for City, but he was given too much space to shoot from 25 yards out and fired the ball into the top corner, although the fact he slipped when connecting with it undoubtedly allowed him to get greater lift on the shot.

With the tie now level, Liverpool responded well. Hart blocked Adam's shot at his near post and Joleon Lescott was forced to make a last-ditch clearance to deny Kuyt after Adam had curled in a glorious cross.

From the resultant corner, Micah Richards blocked Daniel Agger's shot with his outstretched arm and referee Phil Dowd awarded Liverpool a penalty.

With the ball having flicked off Richards' foot first, City's players protested - as did Roberto Mancini afterwards - although it was an identical incident to a handball the City boss felt they should have been given against Manchester United's Phil Jones during their FA Cup defeat. He can't have it both ways.

"Joe is always having a bit of banter and trying to get in your head just before you take a pen," said Gerrard in the official matchday programme ahead of the game. "I just tried to get back in his head. I won the mental battle in the first leg, but that could change tonight. Penalties are very difficult."

The Liverpool captain didn't make it look difficult. He dispatched the ball to Hart's right to win the mental battle again.

Mancini abandoned his formation at half-time, bringing Sergio Aguero on for Savic and reverting to 4-4-2, but if anything it created more space for Bellamy, and Jordan Henderson playing behind him, to run into.

Hart pushed out Kuyt's powerful effort in the 48th minute and shortly afterwards produced the save of the match when he somehow turned Martin Skrtel's shot over.

He was at it again in the 54th minute. Henderson's incisive pass released Kuyt down the right and from his cross, Downing volleyed back across goal only for Hart to spread himself and deflect the ball wide.

It looked only a matter of time before Liverpool would score, but then they were hit by a 67th minute City sucker-punch. Silva fed Kolarov down the left and from his curling, powerful cross Dzeko turned the ball into the net.

With away goals counting double after extra-time, Liverpool had to score again. And they did after Kuyt forced Lescott into conceding a throw-in deep in his own half. Kuyt then fed Bellamy who created space for himself behind Richards by playing a one-two with Glen Johnson and curled the ball with his left foot into the Kop net.

The celebrations were wild. Liverpool were 16 minutes away from Wembley and, in truth, never looked like conceding again.

Substitute Adam Johnson forced Reina into a comfortable save, and Aguero's overhead-kick was easily held by the Reds keeper, but that was all City could muster.

With 94 minutes on the clock, Dowd blew the final whistle and Anfield erupted with a rousing chorus of 'we love you Liverpool, we do' ringing around the ground.

It's not Liverpool's first cup final in 16 years - Cardiff, Dortmund, Istanbul, Monaco, Tokyo and Athens have all been visited in the meantime - but it is our first return to the redeveloped ground that became known as Anfield South in the 1970s and 1980s. What's more, it meant Kopites could finally dust off an old favourite and sing it with pride.

We're on the march with Kenny's army, we're all going to Wem-ber-ley...

LIVERPOOL (4-2-3-1): Reina, G Johnson, Jose Enrique, Agger, Skrtel, Gerrard, Adam, Downing, Kuyt (Carroll 90), Henderson, Bellamy (Kelly 88).
Subs not used: Doni, Maxi, Coates, Carragher, Shelvey.

MAN CITY (3-2-4-1): Hart, Richards, Savic (Aguero 46), Lescott, Barry, De Jong (A Johnson 78), Zabaleta, Kolarov, Nasri, Silva, Dzeko.
Subs not used: Pantilimon, Milner, Hargreaves, Clichy, Rekik.

REFEREE: Phil Dowd (Stoke)
BOOKED: Liverpool: Gerrard (5, foul), Jose Enrique (64, foul), **Manchester City:** Kolaraov (56, foul).
ATTENDANCE: 44,590

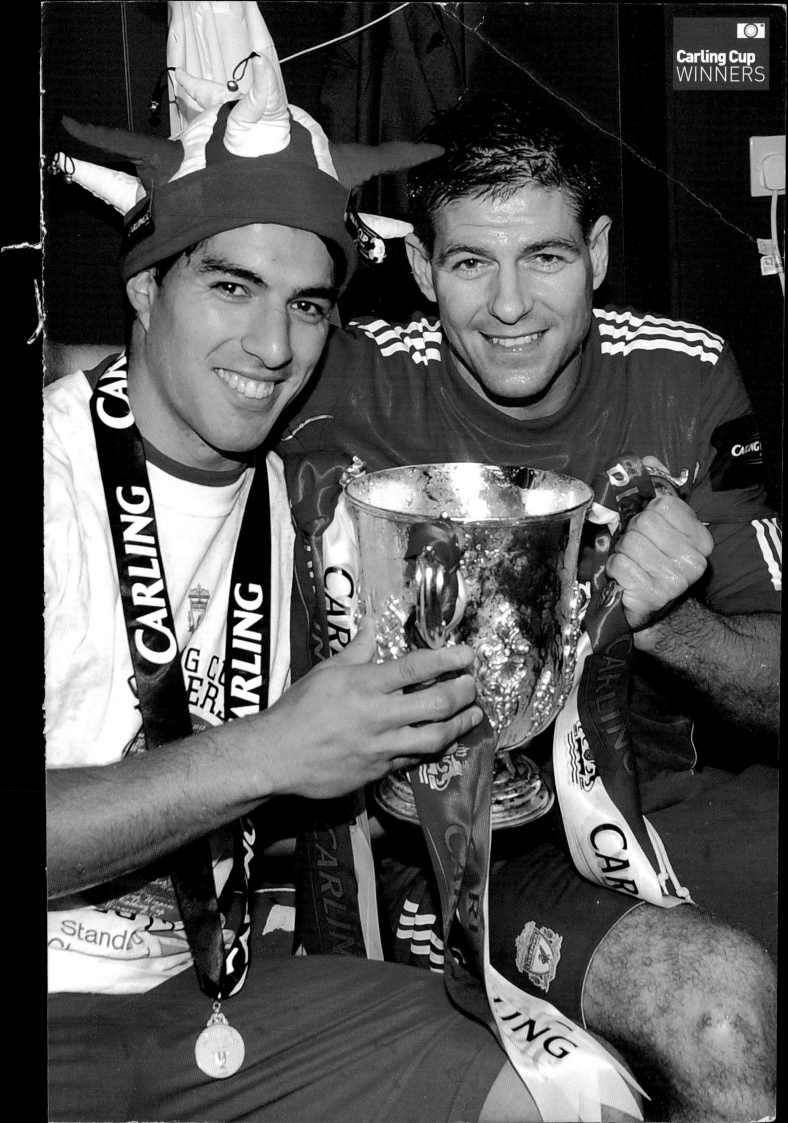

If you've been on the march with Kenny's army to Wembley or following from far afield then you'll want to celebrate Liverpool FC's record eighth League Cup final victory with our Official Winners Souvenir Magazine. Packed with all the cup final action, reaction, analysis, photos, quotes and road trips en-route to Wembley, **'Liverpool FC – Carling Cup Winners 2012'** is a must-read for every Red.

£3.99

ISBN 978-1-908695-11-6

9 781908 695116